Designed to support developmental assessment of twos

What does it mean to be two?

What every practitioner needs to understand about the development of two-year-olds

Jennie Lindon

Updated in accordance with the 2012 Early Years Foundation Stage

Contents

Published by Practical Pre-School Books, A Division of MA Education Ltd,
St Jude's Church, Dulwich Road, Herne Hill, London, SE24 0PB.

Tel: 020 7738 5454

www.practicalpreschoolbooks.com

© MA Education Ltd 2012

All images © MA Education Ltd., other than the images listed below. All photos other than the below taken by Lucie Carlier and Ben Suri.
Front cover image: © iStockphoto.com/coloroftime

ISBN 978-1-907241-38-3

Focus on two-year-olds

What does it mean to be two? explores the developmental needs and likely skills of two-year-olds. The approach and ideas of this book are relevant to practitioners who are working with twos anywhere in the UK. However, the structure of the book follows the statutory framework for England of the Birth to Five Early Years Foundation Stage (EYFS). This new edition of *What does it mean to be two?* has been updated following the revised framework, to be implemented from September 2012. The main EYFS documents can be accessed through the Department for Education website (details on page 56). At the time of writing, Scotland is the only other nation in the UK which has specific guidance about best practice with under-threes (Learning and Teaching Scotland, 2010).

A learning journey across early childhood

In England, early years practitioners have been working within the EYFS since September 2008. The revised statutory framework and supporting guidance are much reduced in length and some details, like the early learning goals for the end of the stage, have been changed.

Of course, everyone has to become familiar with the revised framework. Yet, early years provision with established best practice will not need to make sweeping changes to their approach to children and families. The crucial elements of best practice have not changed.

One focus of change is that the six areas of learning from the first EYFS framework have become seven areas, divided into three **prime** and four **specific** areas. This framework is one way of considering the breadth of children's learning. But of course children do not learn in separate compartments; the whole point is that children's learning crosses all the boundaries. The overall aim of identifying particular areas of learning is still to ensure that early years practitioners do not overlook important areas of development.

The rationale for identifying three prime areas of learning is that secure early development rests upon:

● Communication and language

● Physical development

● Personal, social and emotional development.

These three areas are identified as, *'particularly crucial for igniting children's curiosity and enthusiasm for learning, and for building their capacity to learn, form relationships and thrive'* (DfE, page 4, 2012). The order above is the one given in the EYFS framework. I have moved personal, social and emotional development (PSED) to the front of the list for all the books in the *What does it mean to be…?* series. In terms of child development, it makes more sense to start with the crucial underpinning of PSED.

There is a sound developmental basis for arguing that, without secure personal, social and emotional development, young children spend considerable energy striving for affirmation that they are accepted and loved for themselves. Concern has grown over the shaky communication skills of some young children, whose early experiences have not supported their development. Children's ability and motivation to be an active communicator creates the opening door for other aspects of their development. Making physical development a prime area is also welcome, since this aspect of how young children learn has sometimes been undervalued. Young children need to have easy opportunities to be physically active, encouraged by adult play partners who do not try to curb natural exuberance. There is good reason to be concerned about the well-being of young children whose limited opportunities for active play have already pushed them into sedentary habits.

The guidance for early years practice is that the three prime areas should be uppermost in the minds of practitioners working with younger children. The age range has not been made specific, although the implication is that this strong focus applies to working with under-threes. The further four specific areas are still of relevance for younger children:

● Literacy

● Mathematics

● Understanding the world

● Expressive arts and design.

As the months and early years pass, it is expected that practitioners will focus their attention more evenly across all seven areas. However, throughout early childhood, practitioners need to be very alert to the prime areas, as the basis for successful learning within the four specific areas. If young children are struggling within one or more of the prime areas of development, then the main focus must be there: on identifying the nature of the problem and how you can best help children, in partnership with their family.

'Early Education' (2012) was commissioned by the DfE to produce the supporting non-statutory guidance across the Birth to Five age range. This document explains the four main themes of the EYFS: A Unique Child, Positive Relationships,

Enabling Environments and how they contribute to the fourth theme, Learning and Development. The guidance also includes a revised version of 'Development Matters', cut back in line with the much reduced number of early learning goals (ELGs) for the end of the EYFS. This material offers ideas about how supportive practitioners behave with babies and children and what they could provide within the learning environment. These suggestions should refresh and inform best early years practice. They are not a have-to-do checklist.

The document provides some developmental highlights for a child's journey towards the early learning goals. This resource continues with the previous EYFS approach of broad and overlapping age spans: birth to 11 months, 8-20 months, 16-26 months, 22-36 months, 30-50 months and 40-60+ months. The developmental information is a reminder of the kinds of changes likely to happen, if all is going well with babies and young children. They are, for instance, a brief reminder of the early part of the learning journey towards literacy or numeracy. The items are not an exhaustive list of everything that happens.

As with the first EYFS framework, these developmental highlights and linked practical advice were neither developed, nor intended to be used, as a checklist to assess children. Their value is dependent on the secure child development knowledge of practitioners using the resource. The aim is to refresh realistic expectations, supporting practitioners to focus on the uniqueness of individual babies and children

and to protect the time for them to enjoy secure learning over early childhood. There should be no headlong rush to get twos into the 'older' age spans, let alone the final ELGs. Managers and practitioners all need to understand that none of the descriptions, with the sole exception of the ELGs, are required targets to be observed or assessed.

Child-focused observation and assessment

The revised EYFS continues to highlight the importance of ongoing observation, which enables practitioners to shape learning experiences that are well attuned to the interests and abilities of individual babies and young children. The revised statutory framework stresses that much of this observation arises within day-by-day alert looking and listening. Some practitioners call this informal or incidental observation and sometimes, not always, it may be captured with a brief written note or a photo. All children should have a reliable and descriptive personal record, which will include some more organised observations. The revised EYFS gives very clear direction that, the process of observation and assessment *'should not entail prolonged breaks from interaction with children, nor require excessive paperwork. Paperwork should be limited to that which is absolutely necessary to promote children's successful learning and development'* (DfE, page 10, 2012).

The situation continues to be that, except for the EYFS profile, there are no statutory written formats for observation and assessment, nor for any kind of flexible forward planning. Early years settings and childminders can continue to use approaches that have worked well so far. The only difference is that layouts will need to be changed in line with the seven areas of development. Established best early years practice is not challenged by the revised EYFS framework.

Attentive and knowledgeable key persons will continue to be aware, and keep some records of, the progress of individual children over time. Observant practitioners will learn from watching, listening and being a play partner to children. These observations, often acted upon but not written down, will make a difference to the detail of what is offered to individuals and to sensible short-term changes in planned opportunities for a group of children. Flexible, forward planning will continue to be responsive to the needs and interests of individual babies and children – through continuous provision (the learning environment) and flexible use of planned activities.

The revised EYFS still applies to the end of the reception year at which point children are assessed through a revised EYFS Profile. The total number of early learning goals (ELGs) has been significantly reduced from 69 to 17, and with some different wording. All the ELGs apply to the end of the phase of early childhood: specifically to the level of progress expected by the end of the summer term of the academic year in which a child reaches five years of age. It would make no developmental sense to attempt to apply any ELGs to twos.

Assessing the developmental progress of two-year-olds

The revised EYFS has introduced a new element to the statutory requirements for early years provision. From September 2012 there must be a descriptive individual assessment within the year that children are two: a two-year-old progress check. All early years provision with two-year-olds must organise this developmental assessment. The Early Childhood Unit of the National Children's Bureau (2012) was commissioned to produce non-statutory guidance to support undertaking this statutory assessment. The document 'A Know How Guide: the EYFS Progress Check at Age Two' (see page 56 for references) explains the nature of the check, principles of good practice and a few examples of how the check might be done. These are possibilities and not required *pro formas*. The statutory EYFS framework does not require a set written format for the two-year-old progress check.

Managers, their staff and childminders need to use their professional judgement and can definitely continue to use existing records that will do the job well. The only proviso is that any observation and assessment materials will need to be reorganised in line with the three prime and four specific areas of development. Existing best early years practice should have established a pattern that any written observation includes descriptive examples to support the assessment of existing skills or concerns. These actual examples will, in their turn, inevitably highlight what this child likes, perhaps dislikes and his or her particular interests within play, personal and daily routines or conversation.

The two-year-old development progress check has to focus on the three prime areas, covering the strands within each area (for further guidance see page 52):

● Personal, social and emotional development: self confidence and self awareness; managing feelings and behaviour; making relationships

● Communication and language: listening and attention; understanding; speaking

● Physical development: moving and handling; health and self care.

Practitioners are expected to use their professional judgement over how much to include about this child's progress within the four specific areas of development. The key person will produce a short written summary for each individual two-year-old.

Usual good practice for ongoing observation of children should inform much of the two-year-old progress check. You will have this information as part of the records you keep of all individual children, and which you already will be sharing with their parent(s). However, that information should be brought together in a slightly more formal way as a dated report that gives a summative assessment of this young girl or boy at this time.

● More, of course, will happen after the summary of the progress check has been written. Do not fret about this natural, continued pattern of development. A summative assessment is a snapshot in time. The point is to summarise skills and understanding which this child shows consistently (not fleetingly), and independently (without heavy hints or directive help).

● There will be no need to re-check abilities that are already part of your ongoing observation and assessment of a child. However, the progress check can be a time to ensure that you have noticed important skills or patterns of behaviour.

● An honest assessment can still give a sense of emerging skills and of knowledge or understanding that are recent for this young child. It may also be the time to realise, in partnership with parents, that despite your efforts with encouraging play opportunities, this two is still very unsteady on her feet and looks more like a wobbly young toddler than a child.

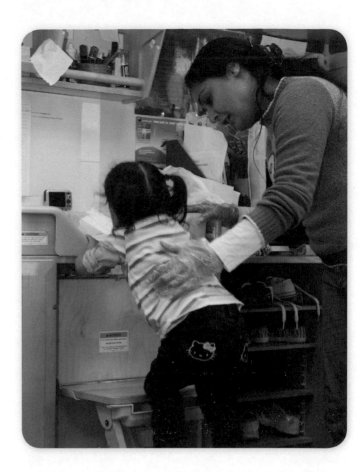

The descriptive report should highlight this child's strengths in development: a can-do focus. However, an honest assessment should be made of any ways in which this child's progress is at a slower pace than is appropriate to expect for her or his age. The progress check has been made statutory because children are more effectively helped when any problems are identified at a young age and addressed.

● It does children no favours for a key person to feel so worried about upsetting a parent that nothing is said about developmental concerns. For instance, usually a two-year-old shows interest in other children – older and younger as well as their peers. The prevalence of happy playing alongside in this age group does not mean twos never make a playful move towards their peers. It is not usual development for twos to be socially uninterested.

● It is important that this summative assessment is clearly dated: a just two-year-old is at a very different stage of development from a nearly three-year-old. A professional concern about being alert to the need for early intervention, when necessary, has to be based on different realistic expectations for a young two, compared with a rising three-year-old.

● The report should describe the activities or strategies which the key person plans to use in order to address any concerns about this child's development. If there are significant concerns, then the key person (with appropriate support) needs to develop a clear plan for how to support the child, drawing on the expertise of other professionals.

- Some two-year-olds will already have a diagnosis of a disability or chronic health condition that affects their developmental progress. In this case the key person needs to discuss with the parent(s) how best to incorporate the insights of other involved professionals – whilst keeping the progress report relatively brief. The aim is not to produce a lengthy report.

The summary of this written review of children's progress should be shared in a conversational meeting with the child's parent(s), or other main family carer. The aim is that the summary can be used to support the child's learning at home. Best practice in partnership with families should ensure that the key person is already knowledgeable about the ways in which this family supports their two-year-old's learning at home. Insights from parents, or other family carers can be part of the progress check.

In some cases, the key person may be able to share realistic expectations for twos and discuss how parents could support learning at home, in ways that they do not already or possibly had not considered. This conversation will need to rest on respect of how children learn within the family and a two-way process of exchange of insights about this child. It would not be good practice for any manager or practitioner simply to tell parents to replicate a list of activities from the nursery day.

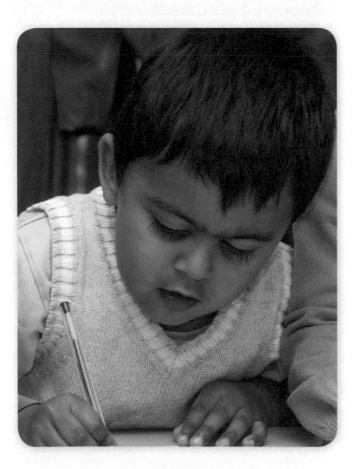

The progress check must be undertaken within the year that children are a two-year-old – so definitely completed before their third birthday. The sensible aim expressed in the EYFS is that, if at all possible, the progress check should be timed to dovetail with the two-year-old health and development review made by health visitors. This assessment, part of the Healthy Child Programme, should happen soon after a child's second birthday: so children are still young two-year-olds.

Individual circumstances will change cases, so there is scope for your professional judgement, in consultation with the family, as to when you gather the information for the progress check and write the report. It would be unwise to proceed regardless with an assessment just to make it fit the timing of the health visitor's assessment. It will not be helpful if your report reflects a young two who was not at ease in your provision and had not come to know you well.

Health visitors or doctors bring their knowledge and professionalism to any developmental check. However, for many families the health visitor will not be a familiar figure to the child, nothing like you as an established key person. Also, this professional is unlikely to see the child in the many different situations that are part of daily life with twos.

- Any two-year-old would need to be settled and at ease within the provision where the check will be made and written.

- Perhaps very young twos have left another form of early years provision to join you. Then best early years practice is that the key person learns about this child from the insights of the previous key person or childminder, as well as from the family.

- Effective partnership with parents and friendly communication is the way to show that this talking between professionals is motivated by your keen wish to do well by their child.

- If a child is experiencing a transition between forms of provision within this year, then practitioners from both places, and the parents, need to decide who will complete the check.

- If a child attends more than one early years setting within a normal week, then a similar three-way discussion needs to happen.

- Generally speaking, the progress check would be completed in the provision (setting or home of a childminder) where this young boy or girl spends most of their week, or will spend most of the year that they are two.

- Whenever more than one form of early years provision is part of the year when children are two, best professional practice would be to include insights from the key person who is not doing the progress check.

Sound knowledge of child development

The effectiveness of the two-year-old progress check is highly dependent on the key person's child development knowledge. Practitioners must have realistic expectations for twos – whether young twos, in the middle of the year or rising threes.

In their own way, two-year-olds are competent and articulate learners. So, as their older selves might announce, it is 'really unfair!' that this group has sometimes been treated as if they are the awkward age: falling between babies and the over threes. If practitioners' child development knowledge is stronger for over threes, then very young children can end up as two-year-old square pegs jammed into three- or four-year-old round holes.

Well-informed practitioners, fully supported by their manager, need to be adept at recognising and respecting a wide range of skills and understanding in the two-year-old version.

- For instance, twos can definitely concentrate but their intense attention looks different from their four-year-old selves. The concentration skills of neither age group should be judged against their willingness to focus fully on what the adult believes to be most important.

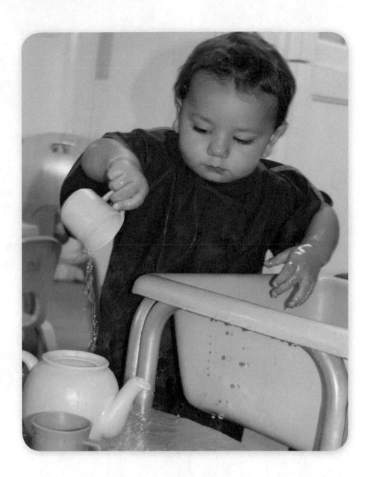

- Likewise, if all is going well, then the chosen play of two-year-olds has extended into the flight of imagination that supports pretend play. However, their patterns of pretend will not be the extended role play of threes and fours. An accurate assessment of twos will be undermined – not to mention their daily well-being – if the creative thinking of this age group is judged to fall short of an arbitrary standard of how 'proper' pretend play should appear to the adult observer.

Sound child development knowledge can be supplemented by the 'Development Matters' guidance materials mentioned on page 3. These developmental highlights are intended to remind and provoke further ideas about what you may have noticed and pointers for what you could be alert for in your daily practice.

- In terms of the overlapping age bands, you will mainly look at the 22-36 months span.

- If you spend your days with older twos, or young children whose development is progressing very well, then the 30-50 months band could become relevant.

- Alternatively, if you are responsible for twos whose experience so far has not been at all favourable, then you look more at the 16-26 months age band.

- This band might also be the most relevant for twos who are already known to have a disability – although

it depends on the nature and severity of the disability. You might need to use different age bands, depending on the developmental focus. Key persons will have to use their professional judgement.

Some two-year-olds will join you with their family already having a clear understanding, possibly a diagnosis, of how a disability is affecting their child's pattern of development. Usual good practice for partnership applies: you talk with parents to understand their child as an individual with familiar routines, likes and dislikes. Parents will be able to tell you, as a childminder or the child's key person in nursery, about their child's current ability level and any special help that will be needed.

You are not expected to know everything about every disability. Good practice is to know how to find out more. Parents will be experts about their own child but may not necessarily have had much help so far, especially if their young child's disability was not apparent until recently. In a group setting the SENCO should have more specialised knowledge and local contacts.

Personal, social and emotional development

The adult responsibility across early childhood is to support young children to build a positive sense of themselves. A secure sense of self esteem can definitely co-exist for children with a realistic outlook on what they can currently do and what is a bit of a struggle. Even the youngest twos are no longer 'babies', and it does them no favours if parents or practitioners treat them that way.

Twos are very young children, yet they have learned a great deal since their baby year. They still need and deserve a lot of support, securely resting on adult willingness to tune into what it feels like to be a two-year-old and an active respect for noticing skills as they will appear in two-year-old style.

You need to tune-in to the likely perspective of two-year-olds and start where they are. What might just-twos say? What does it mean for me to be two?

● Do you still like me, whatever I have done today?

● I am independently mobile, so let me use my skills. I concentrate perfectly well on the move and outdoors.

● I like a chat, so please be patient while I get my thoughts in order.

● While I'm a young two, you probably won't understand everything I say.

● If I look puzzled, it's because your words don't make sense to me – try again more simply, or show me.

● I like getting my hands on nice play materials and I like people to join in my play – that includes you.

● Sometimes I really want to do it myself. But some of my self-care skills are a long-term, joint project.

● Do you keep me in your mind when we are apart?

● I like you to be my safety net, but I need adventures.

● I need to know that a cuddle is on offer whenever I want one.

From your observation of twos, what would you add to this list?

The personal needs of twos

Young and older twos still need significant support with their physical care. Their well-being will be compromised by an unacceptable perspective that care and caring are somehow second best. Care, or nurture if you prefer, is at the core of best practice with all young children. However, a throwaway 'just care' outlook is especially negative for under-threes. An increased concern about the well-being of twos from vulnerable families has further highlighted that quality of experiences really matter for the personal and emotional development of this age group.

The twelve months between being a 'just two' and a 'nearly three' bring a striking developmental difference. Young twos are not smaller, wetter, less articulate threes: they are at a qualitatively different point in their development. I learned a great deal by talking with teams who had lowered their minimum age from three to two years of age. I asked how their practice had adjusted to the developmental needs of twos and these were the valuable observations they shared.

● Settling into a group could be much harder with the twos – both for the child and parent. Of course, separation is not simply a cheery wave goodbye for many over-threes, but the process is much tougher for many two-year-olds.

● Some settings were full of movement and sound and could be overwhelming for very young children. Making adjustments to deal with noise level and creating smaller spaces supported the less sure threes and fours as well. Such changes often helped attention and listening across the age range.

● All twos, but especially the young twos, need time and help with their personal care routines. These very young children are unlikely to be able to manage all their dressing, undressing and personal hygiene. They are in the process of learning self-care skills, including toilet training.

● Twos often want to 'do it myself' and so need familiar adults to show the qualities of patience that they often ask in their turn of the children. However, some parents are still doing practically all of their child's care, possibly for the unwise, short-term adult reason that 'It's quicker if I do it'. So partnership is also a key issue.

● Twos need intimate personal care and this basic need challenges assumptions, if they exist, about, 'we don't change children' or 'we don't wipe bottoms'. Quality

provision cannot be maintained unless young children's toileting needs are met and that means accepting that good care involves close, respectful physical contact.

● The average two-year-old is smaller in stature than threes and fours. This difference is sometimes enough that the youngest children cannot manage some furniture or bathroom fittings. The practical problem was often solved through getting a safe set of little steps.

● Small twos may have to stretch up and over some styles of water or sand trolleys. If the equipment cannot be lowered, the practical answer is to offer natural materials in smaller containers, such as bowls or trays.

● Twos are at a noticeably different stage with their communication skills. Reflective practitioners have described that they needed to adjust the way they talked with these younger children. Adults needed to allow more tuning-in time to understand two-year-olds' expressive skills.

● All the twos, especially the young ones, needed much more emotional support and special objects to be respected like their cuddlies or a blanket. If twos came with a dummy, then it was considerate to take time in coaxing young children to give up this item. It was important to make this effort, sometimes after explaining the reason to parents. It is harder to understand what twos are saying if their mouth is full of dummy, or a thumb.

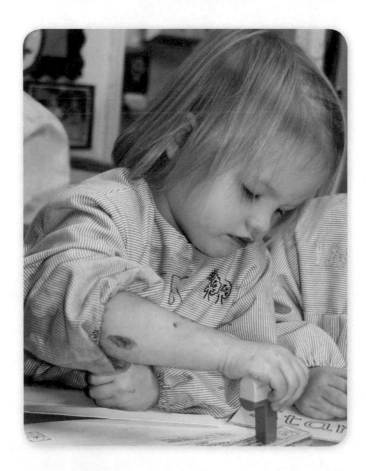

PARTNERSHIP WITH PARENTS: HOME LINKS

Emotional security for young children is built on continuity between home and early years provision. You help through your friendly communication with parents and other family carers.

- Your early relationship-building with parents shows how you want to understand their child's personal preferences and care routines. You are not trying to take over and change established family patterns.

- Share edited highlights of what children have done during the day. Twos may still struggle to find the words to explain, especially if a happy experience needs some new words. Make sure you give parents the chance to talk generally about what happens at home, and not just about problems.

- Some nurseries and childminders welcome tangible links with home: family photos that are given as much importance as those taken by practitioners, home items on display or part of interest tables, a personal box or basket for children who find it reassuring to handle simple items from home during their day or to look at photos (laminated to last longer).

- Even with support, twos could not be expected to manage the kind of turn-taking that was within the abilities of the threes and fours. As a whole, teams said they had to re-adjust their expectations for a wide range of children's everyday social behaviour.

- Twos were often not able, or did not want, to join whole group story or circle time. This often led child-focused teams to reconsider the timing of any whole group activity and the size of the group. The obvious reluctance of some twos highlighted how some older children struggled with large group activities. Rethinking the organisation of the session, or size of the group, often helped threes and fours as well.

- The twos enjoyed many of the play resources that would be available for the threes and fours. They needed a bit more guidance with some tools, but were keen to learn and simply used good quality open-ended resources, such as blocks, in slightly different ways to the older threes and fours. They did not need a very different set of resources.

Some of these issues still arise when twos are with a childminder in the home, rather than group provision. Early years practitioners within the childminding service need to adjust to the different needs of children within their family home. Even experienced practitioners need to be sensitive to the resetting of expectations that happens when you have recently spent time with threes and fours and then a young two joins your provision.

Positive relationships

The revised EYFS (DfE, 2012) continues with the crucial focus on enabling young children to form close, personal relationships and develop a sense of respect for other people. This development rests utterly on the quality of their experiences over early childhood. Very young children cannot learn a positive outlook on making relationships, unless their early childhood is full of affectionate, familiar adults who show day by day how people who care about each other behave. Young children begin to understand the social skills that ease interaction within the context of sustained relationships with adults and the development of genuine friendships with other children.

Attachment is key to young children's emotional health and their strongest and enduring close relationships should be within their family. However, when parents have a job or study obligations, twos can be with childminders or nurseries for many of their waking hours during the week. It is crucial – a non-negotiable part of quality for early years provision – that these very young children are able to make a close relationship of affection and shared experiences with their childminder, their key person in a group setting, and steadily with a small number of familiar practitioners in a staff group. The revised EYFS has definitely confirmed the essential nature of the key person approach established within early years provision.

A warm emotional environment is vital for young children, but also for an adult's support within working life. If practitioners feel under pressure to keep their emotional and physical distance, then it will be impossible to provide an emotionally safe situation for twos, or any young children. Generous and caring attention for individual young children does not amount to 'spoiling'. In contrast, supportive early years practitioners let young children know that they are definitely not 'out of sight – out of mind'. You can let two-year-olds know that they are kept in your thoughts during the day or session:

● You make comments like, 'Clyde, I haven't seen you for a little while. Have you been busy digging in the garden?'

● You start a simple conversation that lets two-year-olds know that you remember what they enjoyed yesterday. Perhaps you have cleared more space so Simone and her friend can recreate their big bus.

● You have not forgotten that Ria told you on Friday that her family was going to visit Grandma at the weekend. So, during Monday's session, you ask about the visit.

● You can use conversation, photos and little personal boxes of home items to reassure young children that they are kept in mind by their families during their day with you.

Perhaps such emotional closeness raises dilemmas about the professional balance between commitment and detachment. Some early years practitioners are concerned that young children will become too attached to them. Maybe a parent's words or facial expression communicate unease that 'my child likes you so much'. This adult problem needs to be faced because children's needs come first. Two-year-olds will feel emotionally insecure if you distance yourself. Young boys and girls, not just the twos, will take this as a personal rejection.

Fortunately, young children do not have a small store of affection that is then emptied. Parents' reservations need to be discussed and not 'solved' by making it hard for young children to form attachments in early years provision. It is tough, but parents need to recognise that shared care means shared affection – and many do realise this fact. Parents also have to use their home time to build shared experiences that are the bedrock of strong family bonds. High quality matters in early years provision, but should never distract parents from ensuring that they spend enough time with their own children. With the increased focus on support for children from vulnerable families, practitioners need to be aware that, in some families, difficulties during children's very early childhood may mean that close attachment has been disrupted. Partnership with parents may need to be led through every opportunity to support the self-confidence of a mother or

LOOKING CLOSELY AT TWOS

I enjoyed going with Ben (2yrs, 6mths) and his mother to a regular session where a small group of twos enjoyed a music and story time.

The leader of this session had taken the trouble to learn all the children's names and was able to greet children personally, even when they had not been for a few weeks. He then held the attention of these very young children because he was enthusiastic, continued to engage all the children individually and gave them the choice of whether to join in or just watch.

I also spent three sessions with the Rumpus Drop-in group and it was clear that Lesley (the group leader) paid close attention to greeting mothers and fathers with their babies or very young children.

New arrivals were made welcome and parents were able to put their children at ease because they had a friendly explanation of how the session ran. Lesley remembered details about children and parents, so that conversations reflected the talk from earlier visits. She was ready to pull out play resources that she recalled had intrigued a toddler or young two during the previous visit.

CRAVEN COLLEGE

LOOKING CLOSELY AT TWOS

Some families regularly attend the Mary Paterson Rumpus Drop-in. These very young children enjoy an affectionate relationship with their parent or grandparent. But they are also emotionally supported by the active interest shown by Lesley, the leader of the Drop-in, and her colleague, in what gains each child's attention day by day.

I joined the group for their trip to a local park. Over a full morning outdoors together I saw many examples of how the Drop-in practitioners were swift to tuck in behind a child's interest or focus in play.

In one part of a little wooded area there was a log, which Lesley pulled back and up so everyone could see what was underneath. Ellie (23 months) and Freddie (2yrs, 2mths) looked carefully at leaves and then they spotted a slug. Lesley noticed their interest, picked up the slug and placed it on her hand, so the children could see it more clearly. Freddie was especially intrigued and watched as the slug curled and uncurled, although he was not keen to touch it. Colin (2yrs, 2mths) now came close enough to look but also did not want to touch the slug. Both of these twos were able to decide on how they would explore the slug; there was no pressure to touch. Freddie suggested taking the slug, 'put in the bag'. Lesley explained that it was better to put the slug back under the log where it lived. Ellie, Freddie and Colin were now all gathered round and very intrigued to look again under the log, where the slug lived and others too. Ellie and Freddie said, 'Bye bye slug'.

Throughout much of the trip, Freddie had shown himself to be a keen collector of sticks and branches. He had an especially large one which was over half his size. Lesley showed Freddie how to use his branch like a hobby horse. He was enthused by this idea and trotted like a horse saying, 'Gee up'. Then Freddie indicated that it was Lesley's turn and she took her go on the horse branch, saying, 'Gee up horsey'. They galloped about together and after a short gap of time Freddie again used the branch to pretend to be a horse.

Lesley found a feather to hold up and let float down. Colin watched intently and picked the feather back up. There was a happy sequence with Lesley dropping the feather, children joining in with, 'weeeee' and then responding to Lesley's, 'where's it gone'. After keen looking, there were cries of, 'we've found it'.

Then Ellie, who had been watching closely started to pick up leaves one at a time and try to thrown them in the air. She persevered and was successful enough to be able to watch as her leaves floated down.

father, who doubt themselves. Uncertain parents may also be struggling with unrealistic expectations of a two-year-old; perhaps over usual patterns of behaviour or twos' very limited ability to flex to the pressing emotional needs of the adult in this relationship. It will be crucial that early years practitioners – whether in a team or working alone as a childminder – are realistic about what they can do. It will never be wise to attempt a level of support for a fellow-adult that is beyond your time or professional skills to develop and maintain.

It is appropriate to encourage a heightened awareness in the early years workforce of the difficulties encountered by vulnerable families. However, this focus must not build an inaccurate problematic image for twos and their families in general. Alertness to the importance of early intervention has to co-exist with the recognition that, in terms of development and family life, many twos are absolutely fine and their family life is happy. The enhanced focus in the revised EYFS about active promotion of learning at home has to rest upon respect from practitioners. Many parents are already doing a great deal to support their child's development, and in ways that are best suited to family life.

Social belonging and feelings

Twos need to feel they belong – in their own family home, of course, but also in other places which become part of their daily life. Individual two-year-olds need to feel they have a

place in their early years provision – sessional as well as full day care. A great deal of this sense of personal belonging has to be led through the behaviour of the adults. Towards the end of early childhood it is realistic to expect that young children have a strong sense of social belonging: to 'my nursery' as well as 'my family'. However, this state will not develop if children have experienced serial interruption of potential relationships – whether by frequent moves between early years provision or disruption in their family.

Young children's enjoyment of social interaction with other children and adults is a different development from learning to follow the more specific requirements of an adult-led circle time or the specialised environment of the school classroom. Events like this do not in themselves build a sense of community. Over time, fours and young fives can understand and sometimes manage the social behaviour that eases interaction in this more formal group context. In the end fives can be ready to understand the different group rules of a more formal group and develop a positive feeling of 'my class'. These still young children cope because they have not been hurried through earlier developments, missing out on the smaller-scale, personalised, child-initiated interactions that should predominate over early childhood.

In a warm emotional environment, twos become at ease with their childminder and the small number of practitioners who should be part of a room for this young age-group. Led through the behaviour of their key person, twos and their parents are personally welcomed when they arrive and, even if occasionally it has to be brief, experience a friendly goodbye at the of the day or session. Even in a regular drop-in, toddlers and twos are pleased to realise that they are familiar to the practitioner who runs the sessions.

Twos are still very much in the process of learning about feelings and they have limited ability, especially the younger twos, to regulate their own emotions or put those feelings into words. They need attention from familiar adults, who are emotionally literate themselves and comfortable to put feelings into words at the time. Young children learn about feelings within an emotionally safe environment and that definitely means with adults who are at ease with touch and physical contact. Being available to young children in this way is fully compatible with best practice for child protection.

In friendly communication, two-year-olds like to be close. When they feel at ease with their important adults, twos move right in, tucking themselves into your arm or draping themselves over a shoulder. Your accessibility creates emotionally stronger two-year-olds, who feel confident that they are welcome and liked in your setting, just as much as in their own home. Twos who are denied this easy access may accept the rejection passively, but they are just as likely to strive even harder for legitimate attention. These distressed and confused young children are not being 'attention-seeking' and their reaction is not 'unacceptable behaviour'.

LOOKING CLOSELY AT TWOS

The team of Buckingham's Nursery had thought a great deal about creating comfortable, cosy corners in every room. Their aim was that every age group through the nursery had an inviting indoor space where they could snuggle up. Each room team had developed a slightly different space and then watched to see how children used the resources. The practitioners then adjusted accordingly.

The cosy corners were created by draped materials or by using a simple canopy and in one room by erecting a lightweight tent. Cushions and other items completed the welcoming environment. Children used these spaces a great deal for quieter play. They sat in comfort to look at books they had chosen or to enjoy a book with an adult and one or two other children. They chatted in a relaxed with adults or their peers and sometimes just enjoyed sitting and watching what else was going on in the room.

If anyone has 'gone off the tracks' in terms of behaviour, it is the adults in this situation.

Two-year-olds need to feel reassured that a cuddle and other forms of touch are available if they are upset, unwell or just a bit uncertain. Undoubtedly, it can be wearing for adults when a two-year-old is emotionally needy in this way. But young children become more able to cope through knowing that you will hold them and contain their distress. You neither try to avoid them nor jolly them out of legitimate feelings. But twos also need the physical welcome of touch and a cuddle that says you are a safe place, from which a young child can venture, when they are ready, to explore the indoor or outdoor resources of your setting. Friendly and respectful touch communicates: 'I'm paying attention to you' or 'that is so interesting! I'm just as excited about the huge worm as you are'.

There is an increased focus nationally on reaching vulnerable twos. Practitioners need to be aware that some (not all) young children who join you through this initiative will be emotionally needy.

● Some twos may, because of their prior experience, be uncertain about how adults are likely to react to requests for close attention and cuddles. You need to offer reassurance, including a warm and responsive attachment to individual children through physical contact.

● Young children feel more confident in themselves and the people who care for them, when they are welcome to be physically close to familiar and trusted adults. Twos (and older children within early childhood) need to be able to snuggle onto a lap or just rest their head against someone, stroking a cheek or holding a hand.

- The physical environment should also offer small spaces: child-sized places of peacefulness. Young children – not only the twos – need cosy corners with a comfortable floor surface and inviting furnishing and furniture.

Social skills and behaviour

Emotional control and social skills are definitely a work in progress for two-year-olds. They have a limited ability to wait and usually run out of friendly options swiftly within a confrontation with another child. Twos need kindly adult support and a wise use of adult strength to make sure that they do not hurt themselves or others. You can help a great deal by holding realistic expectations about turn-taking for

PARTNERSHIP WITH PARENTS: REALISTIC EXPERIENCES

Look for opportunities to share with parents on how you support the social and problem solving skills of two-year-olds. Many parents will welcome the friendly guidance that the time you put in now will pay off later. Adult behaviour has to be tuned into realistic expectations and that two-year-old social skills are a work in progress. For example, with thanks to the Windham Parent Toddler Drop-in, see 'The Property Laws of the Toddler', which they provided on the wall – an amusing, yet accurate, reminder of what it means to be two.

- If I like it, it's mine.

- If it's in my hand, it's mine.

- If I can take it from you, it's mine.

- If it's mine, it must never appear to be yours, in any way.

- If I had it a little while ago, it's mine.

- If I'm doing or building something, all the pieces are mine.

- If it looks just like mine, it's mine.

- If I think it's mine, it's mine.

You help to modify the 'Property Laws' when you are close by, watch, listen and intervene as a good-natured diplomat before the crisis explodes. Attentive and aware adults can contribute a level of negotiation skills that are way beyond two-year-olds, unless the children have some kind support.

twos in a group environment. You also need to make sure there are plenty of flexible resources that make give-and-take an easier option.

All twos welcome support over routines and transitions but you might notice young children who struggle more than their peers, even with all your help. Two-year-olds make the move into rich pretend play and making social contact with other children. Some twos will always be slower to warm up to friendships. But you should notice young children who have had time to settle, and still appear perplexed by patterns of imaginative play and social interaction that their peers take in their stride.

A positive approach to supporting the behaviour of any young children has to be firmly grounded in realistic expectations. Everyone has to consider what young twos – even those with secure family backgrounds – can genuinely manage in terms of social behaviour like turn-taking. What kinds of sharing are too much to expect, even from the older twos, especially if an adult is not alongside as back-up diplomat and calm negotiator?

Parents and early years practitioners help when they tune-in to the current position taken by very young children and guide them on from there. We do not help by constantly telling them 'You must share' – or other kinds of nagging. Adults need to make sure that there are plenty of favoured resources and this approach usually means providing generous stores of flexible materials. Otherwise, it is hard for twos to wait their turn, or to use their fledging social skills to share out a store. It becomes impossible for young children when their play resources are imbalanced towards separate, bought toys, especially when these are moulded plastic, battery-driven items, which rarely, if ever promote easy turn-taking.

Two-year-olds respond well to the visual message of 'plenty for everyone' when they can see lots of building blocks, plenty of dressing-up hats and bags or loads of dolly pegs and containers. Then you will often see twos spontaneously offer items to their peers. Sometimes the actions are within a game of 'I give it to you and then you give it back again'. Yet, on other occasions the behaviour seems to be motivated by a genuine non-verbal message of, 'you need some and I've got enough to spare'.

Even with plenty of resources and supportive adults, a two-year-old's social skills will sometimes be exhausted and the emotional temperature will soar, along with the noise level. As hard as it may feel, the only way to help children is to show them the kind of problem-solving skills that you would like them to learn. If you are to help two-year-olds with such skills, then you have to understand and use problem-solving skills yourself, and that means committing the time.

Even in well-organised nurseries, or family homes for that matter, young children sometimes resort to raised voices or fists, when they both want the same teddy or wooden train. Two-year-old power of language means that even friends sometimes fall out over what seem to adults to be very minor issues in play. Two-year-olds will not manage the talking-through that becomes possible for four-year-olds, who have had experience and practice with problem-solving. Supportive and patient adults lay the ground work by calmly shifting a verbal or physical argument into a problem-solving exchange. The most practical approach I have encountered is that developed within nurseries who follow the High/Scope method (Evans, 2002 and High/Scope, 1999).

Helpful adults create the calm atmosphere and words that enable twos to allow you to help them problem-solve the ordinary ups and downs of daily life. This approach is a good example of how adults need to set a clear, guiding example of how to behave. This model builds firm foundations so that young children become steadily more able to guide themselves.

- You get close and communicate calmness through your body language and words, using firm but gentle physical contact to stop any hurtful behaviour between the children.

- You behave as an emotionally literate adult by active recognition of children's feelings. Younger twos will have only a limited emotional vocabulary, so you can make simple comments like, 'you look cross' or 'yes, I can hear that you're upset'.

- You invite information from the children with an open-ended question such as 'what's happened here?'. You avoid any sense of 'who started it?' or the question 'why did you…?' which rarely gets a helpful reply.

- With your words, you turn a situation from being a quarrel to a problem that needs solving together. You use a phrase like, 'we have a problem here' and then simply describe what is happening like, 'you both want this handbag'. (In an actual situation that I faced, there were plenty of other handbags, but the two young children wanted the same one.)

- Your words and calming body language all communicate: 'What can we do to solve this problem?' Young twos may not be able to voice possibilities, so you can offer, 'would you like to hear my idea?'. Your aim is to suggest rather than impose a way out. In many cases young children will need your support for this alternative.

Using these skills of conflict resolution takes time, although not significant amounts. It can seem quicker to step in and sort everything out, as if you know who had it first or announce that with all this noise nobody can have the bike. But trying for the quick-fix does not support young children to resolve their own problems in the long run. Also, in the short run, they will soon say that you are 'unfair' and 'never listen' about who actually did 'have it first'.

Firm foundations

The descriptive examples you have read so far highlighted very young children who were at ease with themselves and with familiar adults and other children. Yet, young learning buzzes away simultaneously in more than one area of development. Look back and consider what the observations also tell you about children's physical skills, their interest in, and knowledge about, the outdoor world and how they communicated with others.

It is impossible to imagine how very young children could learn in positive ways, unless they feel cherished by the important people within their life. Of course, children will always learn something; they have been busy learners since birth. However, young children, who doubt their worth to familiar adults, spend considerable emotional energy trying to get a friendly, or predictable, response.

It is crucial that very young children are fully welcome to make a close and affectionate relationship with their key person or childminder. It is right to be concerned if you notice an emotional distance between individual twos and close family members. How you help will depend on the nature of your provision, and your own professional skills. For many twos your close relationship exists alongside the secure attachments that many children have made within their family.

Communication
and language

It is complicated to explain and predict how young children manage the impressive developmental achievement of learning to speak one, and often more than one, language within the very early years. But the consistent messages about how we can help do not point to complex techniques. The best interactions, experiences and opportunities for twos are straightforward. The puzzle is sometimes to work out why practitioners, or parents, do not behave in this way.

Chatty twos

Twos are definitely capable of being skilful communicators and attentive listeners when adults have paid attention to what interests the children. By this age you will notice the impact of their early experiences. Young children need plenty of relaxed opportunities to talk as well as listen. Their language skills, as well as general learning, will be stunted if their familiar adults have viewed communication mainly as

'I talk – you listen' or 'my questions are far more important than yours'. Young children can have experienced less-than-favourable circumstances for communication skills without other social or economic factors that could lead them to be seen as 'vulnerable' twos. Young children struggle to learn to listen or talk with confidence if their familiar adults – practitioners or parents – have felt that life is so busy that children just have to fit into those times when the adult is ready to lead a conversation.

It is normal to observe differences between twos of a very similar age – and not only in their language development. However, a crucial benchmark is that two-year-olds should be talking. Practitioners must not let the weeks and months roll by, assuming that spoken language will come eventually. If young twos show no signs of talking, then you need to explore what is getting in their way. There is the possibility that this individual child has an unidentified disability, affecting communication in some way. However, if young children have not been given communicative attention from familiar adults, then the problem lies with their experiences to date.

If all is going well, two-year-olds have the power of language on their side. They are busy making meaning of their world and their voices can now be as busy as their hands and feet. But they are also learning about the purpose and uses of their language. Their experiences in early years provision shape their understanding just as much as their family time. Twos already have some working answers to important life questions such as: 'Do my familiar adults look like they find what I have to say really interesting?' or 'Is it more important to them that I'm quiet and sit nicely?'.

Not-so-chatty twos

Of course, there is a wide range of individual variation. Some 18-month-olds are already chatty, although most likely not easily understood by unfamiliar adults. Other toddlers of the same age have a limited number of words that they actually use. However, their behaviour shows that they understand more than they voice, so long as adult comments or questions make sense in a familiar context. The slower-starting toddlers may be busy learning in another area of development, perhaps very adept physically. They then take off like an express train to catch up their more conversational peers by around the second birthday.

It is possible to keep a watching brief and continue to communicate with parents.

However, developmentally it is realistic to expect some level of spontaneous speech from the just twos. It is appropriate to be concerned if after weeks, and especially months, an older two-year-old is not making utterances that you, as a familiar adult, can understand. The realistic expectation is for twos to be talking. It is risky for young children's progress if their familiar adults – practitioners or parents – shift that expectation towards the third birthday.

Obviously, it is a different situation when young children show the fluency of a two-year-old in a language that you do not speak. Then you need to gain an idea, most likely from their family, how children are managing in their home language(s).

PARTNERSHIP WITH PARENTS: EARLY PHRASES

Toddlers often have a few words that defy being categorised by grammar. These words and short phrases are from what they have heard other people say. When you know a very young child and listen, then you realise how they are acute imitators. They will sometimes produce phrases that you recognise as your own, even down to your intonation, such as 'ohdearyme'. Toddlers use these imitated phrases in the correct context.

Ben appears in this book as a two-year-old, but I knew him from birth. At just a year old, he started to say 'wowlookadat!' to direct people's attention to anything of interest. He had heard this phrase from his mother and older cousins on a family holiday. The children had taken delight in walking Ben around to show him the natural world. As young as he was, Ben imitated this phrase and then used it accurately to get people to look at what he found interesting.

My own son, Drew, at close to two years used his grandfather's jokey phrase of 'just a minute!' to indicate that he would be available very soon. Drew sometimes said the phrase as 'justaminute-Gramps!', showing his recognition that this was the special phrase of one person in the family.

In a close partnership with parents, the key person will be able to share similar examples of conventional words. Parents and grandparents will be able to share home examples with you. It is important that families realise that – much like other endearing anecdotes about very young children – these kinds of observations are a window onto a child's skills of careful observation, imitation and meaningful expression.

PARTNERSHIP WITH PARENTS: CREATIVE CHAT

Toddlers and young twos do not try to speak in a grammatically correct way. They work happily with what they have and use what Annette Karmiloff-Smith (1994) calls 'pivot words'. These are words, or word-like, flexible terms that are hard to classify grammatically, yet work very well to support young spoken communication.

From the *Baby it's You* project, Karmiloff-Smith gives the example of Rowan at 20 months who added 'me' to create a way to ask or command, like, 'shoe me!' and 'apple me!'. She also describes Jimmy, who at 23 months, used 'nogoin' as a handy negative, for instance, 'nogoin juice' and 'nogoin nightnight' (to bed).

Be observant of twos who are familiar to you and spot their individual pivot words. You will also find examples on page 19 from my observation of Tanith, my daughter when she was two-years-old.

These utterances are endearing and personal to the child, so they are a positive focus for communication with parents. Perhaps you can help parents who feel their child is talking 'rubbish' to recognise that these special phrases are an ingenious tool for communication. On the other hand, you will talk with other parents who are ready to admire the creativity of a young son or daughter's current vocabulary.

It is also important that neither practitioners nor parents continue in the year that children are two with an unchecked reassurance that, although this young boy or girl says very little: 'they understand everything we say to them'. You will not know if this confidence is well supported unless you experiment with using exclusively spoken words to the child, by temporarily removing all the usual non-verbal clues.

It is normal that toddlers and young twos make additional sense of spoken communication by looking closely at your gestures, general body language and where your gaze is directed. They also draw on their knowledge about what usually happens in regular routines and how life works here. Twos can be very efficient detectives and they need this skill to make increasing sense of their world. However, with non-talking twos it will be important that the key person (and maybe also the parents, if they wish) checks whether this young child is entirely dependent on context, because he or she does not understand the words.

In a friendly way and within an ordinary, familiar routine, you need to remove all those clues: look directly at the child and not elsewhere, stop your gestures by clasping your hands or having them in your pockets. Make your request or ask a simple question and then observe if this two-year-old can respond to the words alone. Do they continue to look at you, as if waiting for a hint, rather than indicate that they would like some more apple crumble?

Different kinds of words

Before children are far into the year of being two, the whole question of vocabulary should have moved beyond an adult count of how many words children use spontaneously. Spoken communication is now about what kind of words young children understand and use. It is important to recall how expressive language starts.

● Toddlers' first words are those that name familiar people and objects, such as 'Mama', 'dog' or 'juice', although they usually pronounce many of these less than accurately. They then work out that you use the same word for a picture of a banana or a cat as you do for the real thing. Grammatically speaking, these words are nouns.

● Once toddlers have a fair number of naming words, they start to use words for actions like 'jump'. They also combine two words in a way that communicates doing something, for instance, 'getup'. But the same word format, used deliberately with a different tone of voice could indicate the message of, 'I want to get up – please lift me' or alternatively, 'I have climbed up – look at me!'. Nearly twos and young twos also use words that describe something that has happened, like 'gone' or 'broken'. In terms of grammar, these words are verbs and parts of verbs.

● Older toddlers start to combine naming and action words in ways that make sense to them and which meet a range of communication needs. Their very short phrases leave out any linking words such as 'and' or 'because'. Yet their message still makes sense to familiar adults who listen, watch and take the clues from context and body language.

Fortunately, keen young communicators are unworried about correct sentence construction for spoken language or pronouncing a new word right first time around. They go for it with enthusiasm and their utterances become more accurate and fuller over time, because friendly adults take what twos say seriously, often add a bit and sometimes reflect back the correct way to say a new word.

Once older toddlers have a range of naming and action words, they start to understand the kind of words that add further meaning. They use adjectives that add description to people or things and also the adverbs which further describe words about actions. It is important that practitioners polish up this part of child development knowledge. Otherwise well-intentioned, but unwise adults – parents too – try to get young children to talk about abstract concepts before they really understand the words they hear from you.

- Descriptive words make no sense for young children until they can hook them to a noun or verb. For instance, 'dark' does not exist alone. The night or late afternoon winter sky is dark, a room may be dark until the light is switched on. A word like 'fast' means nothing unless it is linked to an action, such as running fast or the toy car that a child pushes fast along the floor.

- All these words refer to abstract concepts, ways of describing the world and young children grasp them intellectually a bit at a time. They need direct, hands-on experience within chosen play to create a tangible connection for meaning.

- Older twos start to get the idea that some naming words include a whole group of people or things, such as animals or fruit. These category nouns are initially difficult for them to understand. For example, twos often struggle to understand for a while that all daddies are men, but not all men are daddies. Two-year-old mistakes are logical and relate to discovering the boundaries belonging to the use of a word.

It is important that neither practitioners nor parents become anxious about skills that are unrealistic for this age group. For example, young twos should not be expected to know a wide array of abstract concepts, especially if their important adults are trying to push these ideas through inappropriate methods, such as colour of the week. On the other hand, two-year-old language development would usually have

LOOKING CLOSELY AT TWOS

By the time my daughter reached her second birthday, it was hard to keep track of Tanith's expressive language – the vocabulary she used herself in her speech. We had noted by then more than 150 single words. But she was already combining them into many two-word phrases and a few simple phrases with three words, such as 'Daddy do it' and 'Let me look'.

Tanith used a mixture of naming, action and descriptive words. In a familiar context, she showed understanding of more words than she actually said – the usual situation for a just two.

- Her vocabulary included the names of all the familiar people in her life, most of the food and drink she liked, the names for animals she could see in the neighbourhood and those featured in her favourite books. She combined a naming word with 'on' or 'off' – usually to make a request, for example, 'beads on', 'clothes off'.

- She used single words to describe her own, or other people's actions, by saying 'swimming', 'digging', 'splashing' and 'eating'. I observed that Tanith probably used the '-ing' format in imitation of my usual way of commenting to her, for instance, 'you're kicking the ball'.

- Tanith also used action words with other simple words, usually to voice a request for somebody else to do something, for instance, 'shut it' and 'hold it'. It took me a short while to work out that her phrase 'help it' was a request for help, but 'help me' was an offer to help. I understood why Tanith had created these combinations when I listened to myself. I regularly said, 'do you want some help with it?' when she was struggling with her clothes. But when she came into the kitchen my usual phrase was, 'do you want to help me?'.

- Tanith also said 'come too', either to indicate that she wanted to accompany someone or to ask somebody in the family to come and join her where she wished to be.

- Tanith spontaneously used a range of descriptive words. She used 'hot', 'warm' and 'cold', also with the further description of 'nose bit cold' and 'very warm'. She had 'tasty' and 'crunchy' (for food), 'light' and 'dark', four colour words that she used accurately herself, 'gentle', 'sticky' (for her hands or the gluey state of her picture), 'squeaky', 'noisy' and 'big bang', 'long' and 'big'.

moved into spontaneous use of some descriptive words. Twos, whose expressive language includes naming and action words but no descriptive words at all, could be delayed in their communication and thinking.

- Twos will have grasped that people and objects have names: a significant intellectual shift. Children then ask by words or a questioning tone to communicate, 'what's that?'. They expand their own vocabulary by actively learning the words for what they want to say.

- So, over their year of being two, young children develop a significant vocabulary – enough that it should become a tough task to write it all down. They start to understand and use other kinds of words and they are able to link their existing vocabulary into short sentences. They use simple words for position, like 'in', 'off', 'under' or 'behind'.

- You will hear some twos use mainly correct words to indicate a time sequence: 'now', 'later', 'when', 'after'. Drew, at two years, three months, said: 'Baby milk when finished hold her' – a phrase that does not make much sense until you know that he was sitting beside me, while I fed his baby sister. Drew knew Tanith needed to finish her feed. But he was letting me know that, after that, he wanted her placed on his lap for a little while.

- Young children need to hear different words in context, said clearly by adults or older children. Twos will then start to use those words themselves and be able to practise. Soon you will hear the words that link together different thoughts or a line of two-year-old reasoning: words like 'if', 'but', 'because', or 'so'.

- The older twos and young threes have a more theoretical understanding of spoken language. Some individuals can be sticklers for accuracy, when another child, perhaps a sibling, says a name or word wrong.

- Young children even start to grasp the idea of emotions if you use feelings words, like 'happy' or 'curious', in a context that gives them meaning to the child. You can expand a little on what young twos have just said, like 'Daddy bye work'. You need to know the child well, listen and look at her face to make a good guess about whether it is appropriate to say, 'yes, your Daddy went to work didn't he? And you gave him such a big hug goodbye'. Or perhaps her face leads you to say, 'yes, you said bye-bye to Daddy didn't you. Do you miss him? You look a little bit sad'.

LOOKING CLOSELY AT TWOS

Young children are generally interested in chatting – about ordinary and out-of-the-ordinary events. They enjoy and want to have conversations with adults who are attentive and follow the flow of children's interest.

During the day I spent at St Mark's Nursery School, one of the practitioners broke her sandal. The children were interested and I heard a mix of twos, threes and fours chat with her in a sustained conversation. They wanted to know what had happened, why she was barefoot (she had taken the sandals off in the garden), what she was going to do now and when she went home. One child wondered whether she really liked the sandals. The children sounded interested in whether this adult was upset that her sandal was beyond repair. The practitioner did like these sandals, so then children wanted to know would she buy another pair exactly the same and, if so, where?

The questions kept coming and the practitioner answered each question patiently and with good humour. It was a good example of an adult being available for children and going with the flow of what had caught their attention. There was no way an incident like this could have been planned – nor was it. The planning element was that in St Mark's, practitioners were attentive and ready for the spontaneous conversations that are the best fuel for young communication skills.

WHAT ARE CHILDREN LEARNING?

Listen carefully to what young children say and in what context. Their logic will often then become clear to you.

For instance, as a young two, my son Drew was confused for a while about foxes and classified them as cats – an understandable mistake. By two years, four months, he had realised the animals were not the same. He enjoyed pointing to a picture in one of his books and announcing, 'fox, like a cat'. Drew used part of my explanation that acknowledged a fox did indeed 'look like a cat', but was actually a different animal.

Have you noticed an example like this one with a two-year-old you know well? These are valuable examples to share with parents, and encourage them to listen attentively as well.

Young children's sensible mistakes in spoken language are a window into their busy thinking. Parents may also welcome your view that these examples are not evidence that their young child is getting it 'wrong', but much more that she or he is working hard to get it right.

Think about how this very young child reached this sensible mistake. For instance, does she think that a descriptive word like 'tasty' is the actual name for her favourite pudding?

Conversational adults: communicative young children

Speech and language teams have become concerned about the fragile communication skills of increasing numbers of three- to five-year-olds. Primary school teams comment on how a proportion of five- and six-year-olds struggle to hold a conversation or listen well enough to cope with classroom life.

Problems arise in some families where parents feel too rushed to talk in a sustained way with young children and may also allow those children to watch far too many hours of television. Aggressive promotion of battery-driven toys has also tempted some parents to delegate communication to impersonal equipment. However, unwise adult choices affecting young communication skills are not limited to family homes. Problems have arisen in some early years provision, when practitioners have felt under pressure to meet targets and gather evidence. Some individuals, and teams, came to feel there was no time to spend (or waste) in what appeared to be idle chit-chat with children. The consequences can be serious for young children's language development.

Children learn about words, sentence structure and use of language through relaxed, one-to-one interactions with friendly, familiar adults. If they receive appropriate personal attention, then children do not need special language programmes, unless they have specific communication difficulties. Practitioners and parents need to hold tight, or return, to basic adult communication skills and personal attention that help young children to build and extend their own skills of listening and talking. The most effective approach is led by simple patterns of behaviour: not complicated 'communication techniques'. If practitioners are to be helpful to young children, sometimes you have to recognise what stops you talking and listening in the ways that support young children: what blocks sensible adult behaviour?

You will help two-year-olds to develop and feel confident in their skills of communication when you are close to young children; the social basis to conversation does not get established over distance. Young children will show you what is their comfortable, personal space, but that is usually pretty close. When you are chatting and listening to several young children, perhaps sitting indoors on a sofa or in a comfy corner, or on a seat in the garden, let your eyes tell each child in turn 'I'm listening to you; I'm interested in what you're telling me.' A slower, more musical intonation can get and hold the attention of young children whose communication skills are under-developed – either through limited experience or for a language disability that may become clear later.

Some years ago, an experienced early years practitioner commented to me that, in her initial training, she was told that in communication with any under-fives a group should be small enough that you can stretch out and touch each child.

PARTNERSHIP WITH PARENTS: TAKING TIME

It is crucial that mothers and fathers see and hear communicative behaviour from early years practitioners which is well worth imitating. Here are some practical ideas. Reflect on how much you behave like this, as well as how you could communicate these ideas if you were talking with parents: as individuals or an informal group.

● Of course adults need to talk, as part of your contribution to the conversation. However, non-stop adult talk is overwhelming for twos, or for any young children.

● Twos need time to process what you have said and then to produce their response. The gaps may be longer than within conversations with slightly older children.

● You will help by respecting and using what I call 'the power of the pause'.

● If you rush to fill the silence, you risk disrupting concentration. You will also fill the gap by guessing what the child wants to say. You may be tempted to add yet another question or comment, while the child is still working on your earlier remark.

● Perhaps a child remains silent or looks perplexed in response to a comment like, 'are you still busy thinking?'. Then you can ask, 'did you hear what I said?', 'did you understand what I asked?' or 'am I making sense?'.

● It is useful when sometimes you model 'thinking time' for children. For example, you might say after a short pause of your own, 'that's a tricky question. I'm thinking about my answer. Right, what I'd say is…'.

● Sometimes (not all the time) you can model thinking out loud with young children, for instance, 'let me think about that. Now how did we build the castle last time?'. It really helps young children when they are encouraged to voice their thinking in this way.

● The older twos will now ask their own simple questions, leading with 'what?' and 'who?'. Young children need brief answers and, if they want, they will ask you another question.

● Ensure that parents see your respect for their children's questions and that it is alright for an adult sometimes to reply with, 'I don't know, but we can find out'.

PARTNERSHIP WITH PARENTS: HOME LANGUAGES

Some twos are learning more than one language: either starting at the same time, or one language following on after they have a basic grasp of the first.

It is possible that bilingual two-year-olds appear slightly slower than average in each language. But looked at logically, children have probably taken on as much language knowledge as their monolingual peers. They have two sets of vocabulary and basic language structures to learn. It would not be appropriate to judge the language skills of bilingual twos on the basis of just one language.

The revised EYFS stresses that all early years practitioners should be confidently fluent in English. Sometimes it may be possible to allocate a key person who is also fluent in a child's home language, when that is not English. Given the wide diversity of languages in the UK, especially in some urban areas, the key person will often need to learn from parents about the children's skill in their home language.

This important aspect of partnership should run through the usual practice of observation-led planning for young children.

- The two-year-old progress check, required by the EYFS for provision in England, will need to be informed by family knowledge as appropriate.

- Everyone needs to recognise – find out if necessary from parents – and respect what bilingual twos can manage.

- It would be neither accurate, nor professional, to imply that individual twos had 'no' or 'very limited' language, just because they spoke a home language that their key person did not understand.

You can help twos, who are the very early stages of learning English as their second language by using the supportive approach outlined in this section.

- Young children, with whom you do not share a fluent language, will nevertheless be thinking like two-year-olds. They are no longer toddlers, let alone babies.

- You help by linking your words and short phrases directly to what you are doing, what the child is doing or what is in front of you both.

- Bilingual twos can then more easily make a connection of meaning for your spoken words.

I agree with this useful guidance and it applies with extras to the younger end of early childhood. My own concept is that of the 'sofa-full'.

Once you get beyond the number of twos that can happily pile onto a sofa, then communication in a 'group' will not hold these young children. Twos in a group larger than a sofa-full can be engaged, but only with lively singing and dancing. Group time with twos does not otherwise support sustained conversation, because there is too much waiting and too many distractions.

Think again if you are tempted to corral twos, or young threes, into groups for communication larger than a sofa-full – or being able to reach out and touch each child. Can these very young children really concentrate? Do they look interested and engaged? Do they join this activity out of genuine choice, or because they are told to sit here? Do you spend a lot of energy trying to hold their attention or capture escaping twos and bring them back again?

Communication has a strong social underpinning and proper conversation has give-and-take. You need to show conversational skills in action by how you behave with children.

- Show young children what a good listener looks like. Pay attention, ask for a repeat or simple explanation, if you do not understand.

- Make your comments link with what a young child has just told you. If you have reason to change the direction of the conversation then flag that up, perhaps with, 'can I tell you about…?' or 'that reminds me of…'.

- Keep it simple and use short phrases that enable two-year-olds to take in what you say, one manageable chunk at a time. The younger twos especially feel overloaded if your sentences roll on, or several requests are bundled up in one long sentence.

- By all means say a word correctly back to a child, as part of your extension in reply. But do not make children re-say a word or phrase, as this feels like unpleasant pressure. They will listen and reform their words and sentence construction in line with what you say.

- It works well to use a child's own words and add a bit or slightly rephrase. For instance, a child says, 'it go there' and, because you are close, you can sensibly say, 'yes, our bricks go into the big box. Well done'.

- When you introduce a topic of conversation or what could be a new idea, then make sure that young children have a good chance of grasping your meaning.

- You might say, 'I can hear the birds singing' but at the same time you point to those birds in the tree.

Thinking and concentrating

Babies and toddlers show evidence in their actions of thinking, but they are not yet able to voice those thoughts in spoken words. Over the year that children are two, they become more able to use their speech to say out loud what is on their mind. One of their routes for exploration is to ask questions, starting with simple 'what?' enquiries.

Helpful practitioners and parents encourage two-year-olds to ask their own questions. Very young children will persevere in finding the right words, because familiar adults show genuine interest and answer the questions. So, listen to children's questions and try to find a way through when you are not quite sure what they are asking. Two-year-olds' questions tell you what they want to puzzle out today – a far better route for young learning than adults following their own agenda of what they want children to know.

Expressing thoughts out loud helps young children to link their ideas and the flow of actions. Many young children voice their thoughts and comment on their actions without having to be encouraged. Watch twos as they play in the sand or work with play dough. They often say, 'need more' or 'put it here'.

Helpful adults treat a child's self-talk as interesting. You listen to young children as you play alongside them, or are engaged in domestic routines like tidying up. Never tell them to be quiet under these circumstances.

It is helpful to young children when you voice your own thinking process. You do not have to sound unhinged when you behave in this way; young children regard self-talk as perfectly natural. For example, you might be in the block corner with a child and say, 'I think I'll make a bridge', pause, then add 'I'm going to need some more bricks' (you might ask if the child can spare some). 'Now I've built the sides of my bridge. I need a long block to lay over them.' You might use a combination of comments on your actions and those of a child helper depending on the activity.

You should be able to observe plenty of young twos like Freddie, who are perfectly able to focus on their own chosen play, whether building, climbing or enjoying flights of imagination. Twos can concentrate when you look for appropriate two-year-old versions of this skill. In contrast, twos do not show 'poor' concentration because they are unimpressed by large group story time or being required to sit still and be quiet for long periods. It is a different situation when you observe a child who finds it hard to settle to any activity, whether a self-chosen experience or a friendly welcome to join an activity with an adult. Without leaping to any conclusions, you can make informal observations and

LOOKING CLOSELY AT TWOS

In the Rumpus Drop-in, Freddie (2yrs, 2mths) was busy in the tuff spot with a store of sand, stones and trucks. He guided his own play by talking out loud to himself, with gaps in between as he moved about his chosen resources. Freddie announced, 'I'm Bob the Builder', 'I'm digging' and 'we got big rocks, big rocks, big rocks'. Freddie went to show Lesley (the Drop-in leader) his stone and said 'big rock'. Lesley looked closely and commented, 'are you making cement?' Freddie said, 'ok, steady, go' and went back to the sand to work with another dump truck. Shortly afterwards he said clearly to himself, 'making 'ment'. Freddie was busy in the sand, but was also able to keep his an eye on what else was going on in the room. He watched an adult brushing up and then focused back to working with his trucks.

Freddie then moved across to the play dough table, requesting, 'Grandma – help'. He took a plastic knife and cut the play dough into cake rounds. Then he pressed his play dough into a shape.

After a while at the play dough Freddie chose to move on and climbed up the slide entrance to the platform of the indoor climbing equipment. He was physically busy for a while and it became clear that Freddie was pretending to be on a train. He continued in his self-talk to guide his pretend play: 'I'm closing the gate', 'click', 'close the gate', 'I'm leaving now' and then he made train noises, 'chh chh, chh'.

PARTNERSHIP WITH PARENTS: CARE OVER QUESTIONS

When adults – parents as well as practitioners – are concerned about a child's language development, they often increase their adult talk, frequently by asking more questions of the child. The adult thinking is well-intentioned but unwise. Perhaps you are offering support to an anxious parent, or perhaps supporting a less sure colleague.

Help the fellow-adult to look from the child's perspective. If young boys and girls struggle to understand you in the first place, then increasing questions is likely to make a child feel under greater pressure to respond 'correctly'. It is far better to adjust how you talk to make a simple comment, then pause and look expectant. Do not rush to fill short silences.

Even when children's language is progressing well for their age, the best approach is still to ask children questions when you genuinely want to know the answer. Avoid testing questions to check if a child knows names, colours and so on. When you spend time close to young children in play and conversation, you will find out easily enough what they understand by watching and listening to them. Twos often enjoy spotting games led by 'Where's the…?'

talk with a child's parent. The pattern of a child's attention, or apparent inattention, might make you wonder about hearing loss.

Communication – part of daily life

The key message about supporting the communication skills of very young children is to use the opportunities that arise within a normal day. Unless children are known to have specific difficulties with language development, twos need the personal attention of familiar adults: within play, enjoyable local outings, relaxing and watching the world go by and ordinary domestic routines such as mealtimes.

I have placed this example here with 'Communication and Language'. Yet what I observed also highlights other areas of these two-year-olds' learning. For instance, they were learning about food in the practical, hands-on way that makes sense to young children. They were recalling highlights of a recipe that had extended their understanding of how ingredients can change: the rising of the pizza dough. It is also important not to overlook the ways in which children use and improve their physical skills through the regular routine of mealtimes.

WHAT ARE CHILDREN LEARNING?

I joined the Rumpus Drop-in for their pizza lunch.

This group of children had made pizzas, supported by Lesley (the Drop-in leader) and their parents (see page 31) and were able to stay to eat their meal.

The mealtime was relaxed and conversational – and children still ate their food and showed real enjoyment in what they had helped to make.

- The adult language was directly related to what was happening at the time. For instance, the pizzas were dished up one plate at a time, with the warning, 'It's hot'. Several parents suggested to their young child, 'you blow on it'.

- Parents took the chance to reminisce with their young children about the ingredients they had all used to make the pizza.

- At one point, Will (2yrs, 6mths) was having trouble cutting his pizza. He said to his mother, 'I'm getting annoyed'. His mother affirmed with, 'Well done for saying you were annoyed. Because you were, weren't you.' I had heard her earlier directly encouraging her son to use feelings words.

Physical development

Physical well-being and generous opportunities to be physically active are as important for young children as emotional security and a friendly, communicative atmosphere. Twos drive their own learning through physical exploration, getting their hands on interesting resources and the sheer joy of being mobile. They are keen to tackle physical challenges and need caring, but not fretful, adults to watch out for those risks that very young children will simply not anticipate.

Physical activity builds skills

Concern has grown about the very low activity levels of some children and the negative impact on their present and future health. Problems multiply when a sedentary lifestyle is combined with an unbalanced diet, which leads to excessive weight gain. The Department of Health (2011), supplemented by the British Heart Foundation (2011) have produced practical guidelines about the importance of physical activity, with practical suggestions for experiences across early childhood. Much like the concern over the communication skills of young children, the current worry about physical inactivity should lead to serious reflection about the behaviour of some parents, and some early years staff groups. Given ordinarily favourable

circumstances, babies and toddlers relish physically active play and they want to use their current skills to the full. So what, and who, is getting in the way for some young children?

The experiences of twos and their secure development are under threat when adults see normal exuberance and 'getting into everything' as a behaviour problem to be managed out of existence. Some young children will be less physically lively than their peers. However, young children as a whole are not designed to be sedentary. They need to use and extend all their physical skills and confidence in movement. It is not a positive sign, if some young girls or boys have learned to be tolerant of the adult expectation that children should stay still for ages, sitting 'nicely' for adult purposes.

You may have encountered the rule of thumb about concentration that young children can manage a timing of their age plus or minus a minute. When you observe young children who have chosen to engage deeply in play, it becomes obvious that twos can remain absorbed in self-selected activity for far longer than 3-4 minutes. The plus or minus their age rule is much more about getting young children to focus on something that is adult-led and probably also requires them to stay still.

LOOKING CLOSELY AT TWOS

I accompanied the Rumpus Drop-in group – the two-person team, three mothers and a grandmother – for a morning trip to their local park. The children – Ellie (23 mths), Alan (15½ mths), Freddie (2yrs, 2mths) and Colin (also 2yrs, 2mths) – were only in their buggies for the walk to and from the park. Otherwise they were physically active for the rest of the morning. These very young children did not need any persuasion to walk, run, clamber and balance or play 'hide' behind trees and bushes. All they needed were the natural resources of the park, plus adults who looked interested, gave a helping hand if requested and who did not get over-anxious about young children in what was a safe enough environment.

The children loved the little wooded section with a path running through it. They reached a slightly more open area, with a raised bank providing a slope, logs, tree stumps and piles of leaves. Ellie walked up and down the leafy slope twice. She then seemed to have gained further confidence and took the slope at a run, up and down – steady on her feet all the time. Then Freddie and Colin imitated Ellie to run up and down the short slope as well.

Alan chose to take the slope at a crawl. But his attention was caught by the wide tree stump. He clambered onto it and stood upright with a triumphant look. He only had a minor wobble, but his mother was right by. Alan was also keen to clamber onto the larger tree trunk, which lay horizontally in this area. He really persevered and worked hard to get onto the top of the trunk.

Freddie's persistent interest over the morning was to find, collect and carry sticks, some quite big. He also used them as a tool: to pat and tap various tree trunks and to make deliberate marks on the dirt path we were walking. He paused in his interest to join in a game of peep-bo within the branches of a tree whose branches swept the ground to create a 'hidden' inner section. All four children spent time hiding and being seen. Colin had sustained fun going in and out of the tree, and sometimes he gave a triumphant call as he ran out and could be 'seen' again.

In this more open area of the park these young children relished being able to run at speed. They ran away a bit from the adults (not far) and then circled back. It was a safe area for them to lengthen the 'invisible elastic' between themselves and familiar adults.

I have placed this example with physical development because it showcases active and capable twos. But look back over the description and consider now what the children might also have been learning about their local neighbourhood and the natural world.

Once you lift this restricted definition of concentration, you will notice very young children focusing on their chosen resources and staying fairly still to stare and touch. When young children are sitting at their chosen activity, possibly on the floor, then you will often notice that they move purposefully in line with their play. Even when they are sitting still it is not unusual that young boys and girls continue to wiggle bare feet or shuffle a bit on their bottom. They are still concentrating; they just need to move a little.

Young children's healthy physical development depends on adults who value lively activity, much of it outdoors and ensure the time and resources for children to be engaged in sustained, active play. Again, much like concerns about children's communication skills, most twos (or any under-5s) do not need special programmes for physical activity. The exception is children who live with a disability or chronic ill health that affects the usual pattern of physical development.

Young children need to work their hands, feet, fingers and toes to engage directly with intriguing materials. Such active and direct experiences support what has sometimes been called the sixth sense: that of proprioception or kinaesthetic feedback. Young children become steadily more able to notice and interpret the messages of their own body. The word 'proprioception' combines the Latin word 'proprius', meaning 'one's own' and 'perception'. Older children and adults, who have experienced plenty of physical, playful activities, show confidence in their movement. They attend to the internal message so their own body without conscious awareness. However, responding to the proprioceptive feedback has been learned throughout early childhood.

Twos, who have been encouraged to be physically active babies and toddlers, are already well on the way to being confident in a range of movements. The measure of their confidence in the internal messages from their body is that even these young children do not always have to look in order to check their planned movement. Young boys and girls can be confident

WHAT ARE CHILDREN LEARNING?

It is crucial to recall how much the different 'areas' of development link together in daily experiences that support young learning. Twos, who have enjoyed time and space for movement, are also much more able than their toddler selves to manoeuvre their body into and out of spaces. Some of the growing understanding about relative position and spatial relationships is truly a whole-body experience, as twos run or ride through a gap, wriggle underneath the table or squeeze into a limited, cosy space. Apart from the sheer enjoyment of this kind of playful activity, very young children are also extending their early mathematical understanding.

about stretching out to get something or clambering up and over a familiar piece of equipment. Twos are keen to help out in simple domestic tasks. They should be welcomed as part of their learning journey for practical life skills. However, another good reason – for anyone who is doubtful – is that happy involvement in tasks like sweeping, brushing up or tidying away all provide valuable feedback to children through their muscles.

Two-year-olds' growing proprioceptive sense is supported by their enthusiasm for smaller spaces into which they can snuggle. Proprioceptive awareness is also about where our bodies end and the external environment begins. There are many reasons to avoid the unwise practice of making young children sit 'neatly' in groups for a story or similar activity. The significant physical reason is that twos, and many threes and fours too, find it very hard to sit separate from any support through physical contact. They will still move around a fair bit when they are cuddled up against you on a sofa or in a cosy corner. Yet young children look considerably more at ease, and less non-stop 'fidgety', than when they are expected to behave as if they are in a school classroom.

Young children do not benefit from their physical activity being driven through highly organised adult-led games or school-type PE. In contrast, twos and other young children benefit from time, space, appropriate resources and a happily engaged familiar adult. Their physical strength, skill level and enhanced proprioceptive sense are fully supported by easy opportunities to walk, run, jump, climb, build, transport, throw,

kick, chase and so on. Twos and other young children relish a playful adult who shares the rules of 'What's the time Mr Wolf?' or who is happy to lead copying games such as 'Simon says', when children are in the mood. Twos also use their physical skills when they are welcome as an active helper in home or nursery. In the normal course of events, twos should be confident walkers and not be spending significant parts of their day in buggies or car seats. Local outings enable them to become stronger and more able walkers.

Two-year-olds, especially young twos, are still fine-tuning their skills of movement, balance and making their senses of vision and hearing support their physical skills. Some twos will

LOOKING CLOSELY AT TWOS

In Buckingham's Nursery I observed an engaging, repetitive game between one adult and several children, using the small rubber hoopla rings. The adult was happy to keep placing one ring on a child's head saying 'on Chloe's head' and using each child's name every time. Each child balanced a very short while with the hoop on their head or tried to walk a bit. The hoop inevitably slid off and then they wanted it placed back on again. The adult commented simply with 'has it fallen off?' and 'do you want the hoop on again?'. Children often 'asked' by handing their hoop to the practitioner, and also to me – since I was standing close by. Then one child balanced a hoop on the adult's head, more than once. Then a couple of children became interested, with the adult, in building up the rings into a tower on the ground.

Several children were keen to practise their jumping and used the lowest step of the set of garden steps. A practitioner reminded them to jump only from the lowest step and the children followed that rule. They took care in going onto the step, turning themselves round and then jumping, or stepping, onto the ground. One girl in particular had a pattern of words to go with each of her jumps – 'Ready steady' and then 'one, two, eleven'. When it looked as if the jumping game was coming to a natural end, the practitioner suggested: 'Can you jump and then run to the slide?' – a simple, although double, instruction which the children were able to follow.

On more than one day, over a rather wet summer, a fine time was had by the twos as they splashed in the puddles that formed in the side section of the lower garden. The children were lively, able to do a lot of deliberate jumping and stepping in and out. They were also very interested in the water and more than once got brooms and helped with sweeping away the water from that section of the outdoors.

LOOKING CLOSELY AT TWOS

I watched the twos from the Tweenies room of Buckingham's Nursery out in the garden. They made enthusiastic use of paintbrushes and the permanent blackboards on the back fence of the garden. These young children were adept at wetting their brush and making deliberate marks on the board – again and again. They were equally enthusiastic about putting balls into the fixed guttering approach and watching as they rolled – or got stuck (equally interesting) along the different sections.

Over breakfast with raisins and breadsticks the twos of the Tweenies room showed careful looking and fine physical skills in handling raisins and manipulating their breadsticks. Over this same routine, there was some playful sound making, led by children and imitated by adults. A few children made 'bubbly' sounds (when you move your tongue and front lip quickly) and went deliberately up and down in volume. This sideline to breakfast was well handled by the adults – it did not get too rumbustious and children still ate their breakfast.

I also spent time with Ben (2yrs, 6mths) in his own home, where he moved around confidently: walking, running, climbing and managing up and down stairs. Ben used his fine physical skills for drawing and, at the same time, he utilised language skills to comment on his actions and plans: 'Oops! There's some paper in the way', 'I'm going to take this one off' (the paper round the crayons) and 'It's a bit noisy' (when he was doing fierce dot-making with a crayon).

Ben also used careful looking and fine physical skills as he worked with materials for building and constructing. He looked equally carefully at his books, turning the pages and opening the flaps one at a time.

At Windham Parent and Toddler Drop-in, young children could move freely between indoors and the outside area. I watched as Jamie and Sara were joined by Maria in a large wooden rocker. The children could not make the rocker work without help. So an adult kept up the momentum with one foot discreetly on the back of the rocker.

Sara experimented with 'look no hands' by lifting her hands off the holding rail and putting them directly up. She managed to keep her sitting balance and looked pleased with her achievement. She then repeated the feat.

All the children were able to keep up a conversation with the adult at the same time as rocking and keeping their balance. They showed their ability to concentrate on more than one task at the same time.

already seem more at home in their own body than their less physically confident peers. All children need plenty of practice with large physical movement as well as fine coordination. Encourage the less enthusiastic climbers and jumpers with a manageable 'one step at a time'. You will then see if there is more to their reluctance than lack of experience combined with low confidence.

The sense of balance for very young children is also supported by their enthusiasm for lively rolling, swinging and spinning – sometimes under their own steam and sometimes supported by equipment or a playful adult. Children need this rather adventurous physical play because it naturally stimulates what is called the vestibular sense: our feelings of position and movement in relation to the physical environment and of temporarily escaping the pull of gravity and then returning to be grounded.

Over-cautious adults – practitioners or parents – can be tempted to stop the livelier games in which children become temporarily off-balance or a bit dizzy. Observe twos and threes who swing to and fro vigorously, or who use a canvas tunnel to do full body rolls. They laugh at being off-balance for a short while, take a short breather and directly experience being well balanced again.

Do the children look happy in their play, do they have a reasonably soft landing and are they avoiding each other in terms of serious crashes?

Learning on the move

Young children need unhurried time and space to play in an active way, with a balance of their own freely chosen activities and simple experiences started by an adult. The measure of a positive balance between the two is that, unless you have observed the entire sequence, it can be hard to distinguish who initiated a game – child or adult.

Young twos are still in the process of gaining full control over their bodies, but their skills are at a significantly greater level of confidence than their toddler selves. They need time, space and adults who respect their need to be active, sometimes totally on the move. When children are welcome to use their skills, then it is easy for adults to observe many aspects of their learning and not only the impressive physical skills. Besides competence in physical development, what else do the following examples tell you about the development of these young children?

It is important that young children develop competence in the wide range of skills that it is possible for them to learn within their first three years. Yet secure and healthy physical development is more than a list of separate skills that twos can 'do'. They need to become very confident in their ability to climb, pour water, build towers, jump or balance. Adults need to create the environment with time and many opportunities for two-year-old adventures – getting steadily better through self-chosen practice. Young children become more adept at balancing along a low plank, because they have had generous times for practising. They learn to clamber up and jump from a low height because they have had resources that remain steady for their jump and adults who are relaxed within a safe enough environment.

Twos need experiences that support a sense of 'I can' or 'maybe I could' and 'I'm going to have a go'. Self-confidence needs to go hand-in-hand with technical competence. Otherwise, young children have potential physical skills that they choose not to use, perhaps because they feel that what they manage is never quite good enough for the grown-ups. Confidence in very young children is shown partly by persistence, when they keep trying to make a sand castle that does not collapse. In the same way, they make every effort to tell you about the 'big, hairy cat on the high wall', although they are missing key words to describe this thrilling event.

Sharing the care of twos

Continuity of care between the family home and early years provision is crucial for young children's sense of well-being. This means partnership with parents of two-year-olds needs easy and detailed communication over personal care routines. This open communication is best undertaken between the key person and parent(s) or other family carer(s). Young children grow in confidence when they can steadily

LOOKING CLOSELY AT TWOS

In Buckingham's Nursery, twos and young threes were able to sit and focus on their lunch, main course and pudding.

- A calm and supportive atmosphere has been developed by the room team, through having small tables and an adult sitting with each table of children.

- Even the two-year-olds were able to sit for their lunch because they had been suitably active during their morning.

- I watched young children who were enthusiastic about their food and drink and were willing to persevere in using cutlery appropriate for their age.

- Friendly mealtimes are opportunities to see twos' fine physical skills. The abilities are used for good reason by young children who like 'to do it myself'.

- In a warm emotional atmosphere, young children also feel confident to ask for help when they need it.

PARTNERSHIP WITH PARENTS: TOILET TRAINING

It is realistic to expect that, during the year that they are two, young girls and boys become reliably toilet trained for daytime – unless they live with a disability or chronic health condition that complicates this process. Being fully toilet trained means that twos wear ordinary underwear, not padded pull-up pants – never mind what some manufacturers would have parents believe.

This process should be undertaken in close partnership with the child's family. The key person will need to be flexible to parents' wishes about when to start toilet training. However, the onset should not be postponed indefinitely. Early years practitioners need to initiate that careful conversation if parents are resistant. It does young children no favours if they are getting close to their third birthday and nobody has got around to getting them out of nappies. Toilet training is an important example of how care and caring has to be an integral part of best practice within early childhood. Supporting a child through this process, and dealing with the inevitable occasional accident later on, is part of a responsible holistic approach by the key person in any kind of provision. It is certainly not an annoying side issue, to be delegated to colleagues who are viewed as less qualified.

share in their own care and feel self-reliant in an emotionally safe way. Part of their security arises from seeing their parent(s) and key person talking easily together.

The best practice for babies and young children is that the key person undertakes the personal care of their key children. This approach is possible; I have observed it to work in nurseries. After they feel at ease in their nursery, young children accept that another familiar person will help, when their key person is away ill or on holiday. At the very least, the key person must take responsibility through the settling process – however long the child shows that to be – and so is able to become familiar with a child's preferred routines for changing or toileting, mealtimes and sleep or rest times. The key person should still be very available to the individual children but will have communicated clearly to a colleague, at most two, the important information about this child's preferences:

● What can this two-year-old manage and how? Do they have personal words to express their toileting needs?

● What do they need in terms of routine or comfort to ease their transition into sleep or rest time?

PARTNERSHIP WITH PARENTS: SUPPORTING INDEPENDENCE

Early years practitioners need to set a good example to parents or other family members about supporting young children's independence. Parents who allow the time for young sons or daughters to become competent will be affirmed by your practice. Parents (or unwise practitioners) who feel 'it's quicker if I do it', need to be encouraged to ask themselves – what kind of children do we all want to raise for the next grown-up generation?

● Children who feel competent, yet able to ask for help if needed?

● Children who feel they will rarely meet tough adult standards?

● Children who are convinced they have people who will dress them and mop up after them, as if they were a highly paid celebrity?

Adults, who do not give time for children to learn the skills, need to think of the consequence in postponing this learning. When are very young children going to learn crucial skills of self-reliance? The best time to learn a skill is when you can see you need it and are keen to learn. It is not a happy experience – as a four- or five-year-old – to have to tackle skills because adults have now become impatient.

● What is this two-year-old likely to find familiar or unfamiliar about meal or snack times in this setting compared with family life?

Healthy habits and the nurture of routines

Friendly and predictable routines matter to young children. A relaxed snack or lunchtime offers a very positive experience for children and observant adults will notice the many ways in which mealtimes are supportive of a wide range of skills. Twos learn age-appropriate independence for eating and drinking, as well as the basic social skills for shared mealtimes. Best practice is create a happy and social atmosphere, in which it is understood that everyone – adults too – sits at the table for this period of time. So there is even more of a good reason not to squander twos' limited ability to sit relatively still. Twos will have run out of patience for sitting by meal time if they have experienced a day or session imbalanced towards adult-led activities that limit spontaneous physical play.

Young children like to be able to predict and anticipate some of their day. Of course, surprises are nice sometimes, but two-year-olds can be unsettled by a day or session that moves on, or changes, without obvious markers. Caring routines for twos are partly about their continued need for intimate personal care, although they will be steadily sharing in the tasks. Adults need also to value and show respect for the regular routines of the day or session. Young children need to settle into their childminder's home or the pattern for their nursery or playgroup. But even children who are 'officially settled' have times when they are not happy to let their parent go or something has happened to disconcert them.

Twos should not be rushed into premature independence. The delight of 'doing it myself' is severely reduced if help is in short supply when twos struggle, or just feel like being cosseted today. However, two-year-olds can already have learned many abilities and want to use them. If twos are to be able to take over and practise their own self-care skills, you need to:

● Make the time so that young children can practise their dressing and undressing, hand washing and toileting, mealtimes and all the other routines and skills that are best learned within the earliest years.

● Value that these abilities matter and admire what is involved: fine physical skills, sequencing, concentration and a motivation to keep trying.

● Show genuine pleasure at what twos can do and comment appropriately, whether it is 'you've put your coat – all by yourself. Well done!' or guiding the routine by your own words, such as, 'we're going outside – so where are our sun hats?'.

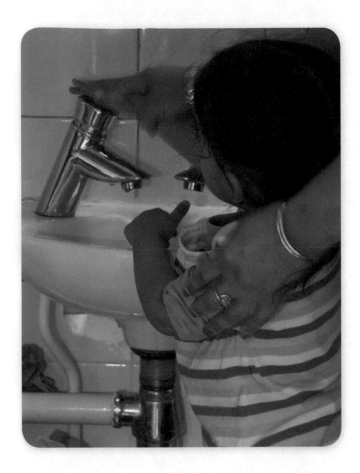

- Resist the temptation to hurry twos and, unless there is a very good reason, let them have enough time to have a go themselves. Avoid the temptation to redo a self-care task like buttoning up a coat or domestic routine to your own, adult standards. It is fine, for twos' own well-being, to ask 'can I put sun cream on the back of your neck?' because the child has missed a bit.

The regular routines of personal care are not something to hurry through to move on to other activities that are defined, unwisely, as more important early learning. Two-year-olds who feel relaxed, who have not been rushed through their personal care routines, will be ready to enjoy play resources in your setting.

Given time and adult patience, young children will share in their own care and contribute to looking after their nursery or home environment. This long drawn-out process is a directly valuable source of learning: for a sense of pride in their own capability, confident physical skills, communication, simple forward planning and understanding a sequence within daily domestic routines.

Physically active helpers

Early years practitioners can use all the opportunities that naturally present themselves. You do not have to design and plan special activities; simply welcome young children as active helpers.

LOOKING CLOSELY AT TWOS

On Wednesdays the Rumpus Drop-in group always cook and eat lunch together. The team then add the recipe and photos of the event to their growing number of cookbooks, which are accessible on the shelf. Today they were making pizza and the enthusiastic group of children was seated round the table, with their mother or father. The youngest child was 19 months and the eldest a four-year-old older sibling. The children were helped to wash their hands before beginning and reminded in a friendly way to wash again, when a couple of them left the cooking table to play elsewhere and then came back again.

Lesley (the Drop-in leader) commented each time as she did anything within the process and the children were hands-on at the various stages. They stirred the mixture with a wooden spoon and everyone had a go at kneading the dough. Lesley showed how to knead and commented as she demonstrated: 'You can fold it. You can pummel it'. Each child kneaded the pizza dough and Lesley commented briefly, using descriptive words like 'pressing' and 'squashing'. Lesley then explained: 'We're going to let the dough rest and it should grow. Then we're going to grate some cheese and make the tomato sauce'.

She passed round an unopened package of mozzarella for the children to feel and asked: 'What do you think it is? Is it squishy?' Some children guessed it was flour. One girl suggested, 'let's open it and see' and Lesley cut the package open and poured it into bowl. Lesley explained, 'It's mozzarella cheese' and gave each child a bit to tear up very small.

Then the children each had a knife and part of a big mushroom to cut up into smaller pieces. Will (2yrs, 6mths) was very adept at cutting – the most competent in the small group. He was able to hold his mushroom to steady it and then slice efficiently with his right hand. I talked with Will's mother and she explained that she cooks with him at home, but had started because of being part of the cooking sessions at the Drop-in.

While the group was working on the pizza toppings, the dough was expanding in the warmth of the kitchen. It had grown noticeably. Lesley rolled out the large circles and put tomato sauce on the dough. She then showed how to spread the sauce with a spoon, explaining 'this is called smoothing'. She showed and explained: 'Otherwise (showing a motion of digging with the spoon) we'll have holes in our pizza'. Each child now had a go with spreading the shredded mozzarella, grated cheddar, cut mushrooms and fresh tomatoes across the two large pizzas. Finally the children put the basil leaves on top, having smelled them and shredded them a little.

PARTNERSHIP WITH PARENTS: BASIC HELPFULNESS

If parents are uncertain about how best to guide their young children towards basic helpfulness, they need a wise example set by early years practitioners. Parents should be able to notice your model of simple appreciation working as the best form of encouragement. Young children flourish when they hear your thanks in words and a warm smile. You may alert twos to the positive consequence of their 'hard work' with, 'that was such a speedy tidy-up job. Well done! Now we have time for an extra story'.

Twos (or threes and fours) do not need to be 'paid' – with presents or treats for ordinary helping out with domestic routines. It is unwise to establish this expectation with young children at home and equally unwise in any early years provision, where the prize is more likely to be a sticker.

Two-year-olds do not really understand the symbolic nature of stickers, or similar forms of reward, although they will not turn them down. However, children will soon ask 'will I get a sticker?' when you request them to take on a routine task. Perhaps you answer, 'no – we all help out here'. Then young children may legitimately decline to accept that task. They are not being 'uncooperative' or any other negative behaviour label. Children are responding to the situation set up by the adults. Their reaction shows they understand that you have established a token economy in your nursery or home.

If you face this situation, it is well worth reflecting how you offer encouragement and show appreciation. If parents have started to track how many stickers their child receives, then definitely do some serious rethinking.

- Twos like to be part of putting out the sleep mats or bedding in full day nurseries. I have seen young children fully capable of joining in this task, and proud to be trusted. Some twos and young threes are also aware that individual peers like to have their bedding or mat in the same place, with a cuddly, or other personal items ready to greet them at sleep or rest time.

- Within drink, snack or mealtimes, cutlery and tableware can all be chosen so that children can help with this routine. Small jugs help children to do their own pouring. An easily accessible cloth lets them wipe up any spillage.

- The timing of toileting and hand washing should enable children to be as independent as they wish. Adult help is always on offer, but not imposed on young children who are managing well enough and wish to 'do it myself'.

- Do not be surprised that young children often find the bathroom to be an interesting place. Of course, this room or area of a setting must be safe and hygienic. But the point of such awareness is that twos do not have to be hurried through a self-care routine that they can partly manage on their own.

Twos appreciate the calm when you give time and plan routines like mealtime, so that everything is close at hand. It will distract children if you bob up and down on a regular basis. In a family home and any group setting you should equip the routine so children can do a lot themselves. Supportive adults also keep to the familiar routine and the layout of the learning environment. You do not change corners or the contents of a resource box, except for a good reason. Then you let children know what will change, with a simple explanation of why. You also discuss with them any changeovers of pictures or photos that are on display; they then feel a sense of ownership.

Sensible planning allows you time to respect a two-year-old's need for personal care and to value their wish to be active helpers in regular routines. Ordinary, domestic events support children's learning in a holistic way. For instance:

- Young children experience personal satisfaction from being a helper to adults and other children. They feel trusted and like the sense of 'that's my job' or 'me and Amy did that'. A friendly atmosphere establishes that 'we all help out in our nursery' (or a child's home-from-home with a childminder).

- When two-year-olds are active in a tidying-up routine, they learn about same and different, what fits and what does not and putting resources back into the right basket or box. Twos sometimes even use creativity to reorganise how materials are stored.

- Young children sometimes learn about working together with another child as a partner, because 'we need two of us – this basket is heavy' or 'I'm doing the plates and Gavin is doing the cups'. Twos are building a sense of community for their little group: a sense of shared responsibility for how daily life works.

- Children's involvement in the routines for snacks, drinks or mealtimes provides a meaningful context to use numbers for counting. Laying the table requires physical skills alongside visual coordination, as does serving a friend with another helping of vegetables.

- Young children often chat when they are part of a shared domestic activity, like sorting out the fruit. They use communication skills in a relaxed, one-to-one context with an adult or perhaps one other child.

Direct hands-on learning

Given time and ordinary encouragement from adults, young children are keen to be active. Some twos are especially keen on using wheeled vehicles. They spend energy and use careful looking as they steer to move forward and back, and sometimes tight reversing. They can also experiment with speed and turning, within their space.

Children's outdoor physical exploration extends their understanding of the natural world. Young children enjoy being involved in simple gardening projects. But they are also keen on the simplest of garden maintenance: the watering. The best option is for them to be able to fill cans up from a low tap on a water butt. They love filling, watering, emptying and refilling. But, with a little guidance, twos can use their physical skills to water specific areas, like a newly-laid section of turf. Adult planning about storage can ensure that even young children will put their watering can back on a free hook.

Best early years practice is to be an easily available adult and friendly play partner. Sometimes you will be given 'orders' by twos who know exactly how they want you to help with this enterprise. Without overwhelming their play, this is your opportunity to comment appropriately within the game or busy activity. For instance, when you are welcomed to be part of digging, filling and building in the outdoor sand area, there will be sensible times to add appropriate words about texture or size, as well as simple advice.

WHAT ARE CHILDREN LEARNING?

In Buckinghams Nursery the two-year-olds spent a generous amount of time out in the garden. They were happily active with a wide range of equipment, but had just as much enjoyment using the opportunities of the physical environment. In the following examples, these young children were honing their physical abilities. What other areas of learning do you think were supported by their chosen play?

- Young children often climbed up and back down the set of steps from the lower to the upper garden, without going anywhere in particular. It looked like an example of twos doing something for the sheer satisfaction of being able to manage that skill.

- Over the summer, I watched several times as twos wanted to jump from the steps. They were welcome to do this, but asked by practitioners to jump from the lowest step. Children co-operated with this request.

- One afternoon there was a lively game as one practitioner and enthused children ran around the lower garden. The adult was calling, and the children took over, with 'faster, faster' and 'run as fast as you can' and 'running, running'.

Literacy

What do early literacy skills look like?

The revised EYFS has divided the developmental area of Literacy from Language and Communication. The two areas are, of course, closely linked, but there is an advantage when practitioners are stimulated to reflect on spoken communication and the skills of understanding language as distinct from the learning journey towards being able, eventually, to read and write.

If all has gone well, then even very young twos have already built some skills that are important for the literacy journey. Some rising threes show that they have the beginnings of an understanding that there is a world of written language.

The current anxiety about literacy has arisen because too many young people have emerged from years of schooling with fragile literacy skills. Some of those adults work with young children. Managers and practitioners themselves need to recognise when staff reading or spelling skills need improvement.

Any written material in your setting should be correct: spelling, basic grammar and punctuation. Early years practitioners need to write up their observations, and compose a clearly written summary for the two-year-old progress check.

Appropriately, there is nothing in the EYFS materials (first version or revised materials) implying that twos might understand, read or write actual letters. However, the normal two-year-old skill base – arising from their play and conversational experiences – includes abilities that are important for later literacy. Early years practitioners need to have a firm grasp of these strands – for your own best practice. However, you also need to be able to explain the process clearly to parents and other family carers.

Two-year-olds, supported by practitioners and parents, can build a strong basis for literacy with the following strands.

- Two-year-olds, even the youngest twos, can be very enthusiastic about books and storytelling. With appropriate early experiences, these very young girls and boys are already familiar with how books work, and they have their own favourites.

- Twos with previous experience of books often choose to select and look at a book themselves, without any adult prompting.

- If children join your provision in the year that they are two, are they bringing an established enthusiasm for books? Some twos will not be familiar with books, or the enjoyment of hearing stories, before they join you. Then, you need to build happy experiences of looking at books, listening to stories and also how to take care of books and storytelling resources like puppets.

- The behaviour with books of some older twos and rising threes begins to look like that of 'a reader'. Watch them and you see that these still very young children look deliberately and carefully across the page. They understand that different parts of a story go with each illustration, or a commentary to books about a subject, like big trucks.

- Twos who are familiar with books also have the concept of when the telling of a story is complete, the book is finished, 'all done' and they may then request the book or story 'again'.

- Young children's request to have favourite stories many times is ideally suited for their learning. The repetition helps them to recall the details, including enjoyable repeating phrases that are part of some narratives. You will also hear some twos tell themselves a simple story as they turn the pages.

- Twos also show a more general awareness of narrative: they try to tell or request that you recount their own personal stories: what happened in the park or how the bird flew into the window with a big bang.

- Children like a story read or told to pictures with plenty of expression in the words and your face. They enjoy dramatic pauses and repeating those phrases that they can say. Enthusiastic listeners to stories will have the motivation to want to learn to read in the future, when they are ready.

- Reading is not just a technical skill of sounding out letters to form words, although of course that will be important. Young children need to build the understanding of how words link together for meaning. Many rising threes have grasped that the text that adults read to them sometimes tells a story, but may also give information about the photo or other illustration.

Rich oral communication is a crucial basis for written language. Twos can already be alert to the sounds of their own language(s). If they are welcome to spend their earliest years becoming adept with spoken language, then children will later be in a much stronger position to decode the written form of the language.

- Over the year that they are two, young children should be building a large vocabulary – and continue to do so – through play and relaxed conversation. Later, when they are ready to read, children will recognise the words they decode from combinations of letters and be able to sound out familiar words that they want to write.

LOOKING CLOSELY AT TWOS

In the Rumpus Drop-in Lesley (the leader) was sitting on sofa with Pippa (2yrs, 5mths) and Will (2yrs, 6mths) on either side of her. They were looking at a song book and both children were looking at the book closely. Lesley was commenting on the pictures in the book and they sung some of the songs.

She asked about one picture, wondering aloud which song it was. Will made the movement of rolling hands for 'Wind the bobbin up' and Lesley said that was a good guess. Both children pointed to another picture and Lesley said, 'I don't know that song'. Will sounded puzzled that an adult could possibly not know any song and she explained, 'I can read the words, but I don't know how it goes. I'll have to find out the tune.' The children identified another picture for a song and asked, 'shall we just do one more?' Lesley explained she knew this song, 'Here We Go Looby Loo'. She then opened another book – a story this time: *Peace at Last*.

Rebecca (3yrs, 3mths) had joined the sofa group and all three children leaned in. Pippa in particular looked very closely at Lesley's face and then at the book. They were all three held by the storyline and, with such a small group on the sofa, each child could each see and hear clearly.

LOOKING CLOSELY AT TWOS

Two-year-olds can be well on the road for early literacy, when their experiences as babies and toddlers have built sound foundations.

In Buckingham's Nursery School, by the time children join the Tweenies room, they are already book enthusiasts – supported also by their positive family experiences. I observed a lively small group story time with twos who enjoyed a book about 'How do you make a rainbow?' and then a different book about animals hiding in the jungle.

These very young children knew how to look closely at the picture and to listen to the words that the adult read aloud. Furthermore, these twos understood the pattern of question-and-answer that was part of this kind of book. Especially with the hidden jungle animals, some twos knew the answer. Other children showed that they understood the pace and tone of this kind of exchange. They responded in a different way when the adult was asking the question from when she was saying the answer. Several children echo-ed the words of the answer, but not those of the question.

I observed as six two-year-olds sat happily on low benches forming a quiet corner in part of the garden – each child looking at his or her chosen book. Soon, an adult with them was 'spotting' items in a book with two of the children. A little bit later another adult was reading a Postman Pat book to the whole small group. One child was aware of the exact pattern of the story and asked the adult to turn the page back to read the last word of that sentence. It appeared that the word belonged on the previous page and the child knew the adult had turned over a little too soon.

I spent time with Sophie (2yrs, 8mths) in her own home. During the morning, she was keen to get out *Rumble in the Jungle*, a favourite book at the time. Sophie understands a lot about books and is happy to share this interest with her baby sister, Lucy.

Sophie wanted to point out some of the animals to Lucy. Sophie became intrigued by a theme in the story about fleas and that 'monkeys eat fleas'. All the time, Lucy was staring at the book, at each page and touching the pages. Sophie held one side of the book to help her mother, Louise. Sophie had learned the names of most of the animals in this book. She enthusiastically said: 'There's…' and pointed and named many of them. Sophie had a good guess for those names she did not know. She did not know vulture, but expressed the opinion that it looked 'like a flamingo'. She was right, because the vulture in this illustration did have a neck all stretched out and pink.

PARTNERSHIP WITH PARENTS: MARK MAKING

It is crucial that parents can see developmentally appropriate practice in your setting. You need to be using wise resources and offering experiences for young children that are worth imitating, maybe with a bit of adaptation, for the family home. Show and share with parents how much their two-year-olds enjoy meaningful mark making. Explain how mark making out of choice is such an important step on the way towards emergent writing.

● Children flourish with encouragement to use mark-making materials, and are happy to use the blank side of paper or card with writing on the other side. Parents should not feel they have to buy lots of stationery, although undoubtedly children often love some special stores of their own.

● Reassure parents that it is fine and wise to set clear boundaries for a family home (rather than nursery) for where it is fine to make marks and where it is not alright.

● In conversation with parents about their own son or daughter, get across the importance of accepting what twos tell you they have done in their meaningful mark making. Rising threes may soon say that they have 'written' something, so it does not sound polite if adults call it 'scribbling'.

● Share real examples of what you do to communicate. Young children need to see their familiar adults as writers and readers within the ordinary routines of the day.

● So long as twos can enjoy genuine conversation with interested, familiar adults, they become confident with using language to explain, argue or recount. They get their thoughts out of their head through their mouth. Writing is not solely a technical skill of forming the letters. When they are ready, children need reasons to want to write and they need to feel competent to get their thoughts in order.

● Again, on the basis of happy experiences (not just because they have passed their second birthday) young twos can show they know a range of familiar songs, nursery rhymes and chants. They show their ability to recall and reproduce the words and the rhythm of a nursery rhyme or jingle, along with the accompanying hand movements.

Respect for children's physical development is a crucial part of best practice with twos. However, physical skills are also a vital strand in young children's learning journey towards the handwriting side of literacy.

- Being able to direct their gaze and look carefully will support children's ability, later, to follow a line of print and to judge the formation of their letters. At the moment, their ability to look as well as plan ahead will be applied to their own purposes for meaningful mark making.

- Twos who have time and suitable simple resources can be enthusiastic in their painting, drawing and free style of mark making. They are learning about how to make deliberate marks, choosing to repeat lines or shapes or blodges. But children are also building an intellectual understanding of mark making – 'when I make this movement, then I can create this swirl or that long line'.

- Some rising threes may also tell adults that a mark is something in particular. The child's confident pronouncement may be about what their painting or drawing represents. However, some older twos have already had the meaningful experiences to grasp some everyday elements of what writing does in daily life. Perhaps they make it clear that this piece of paper with the marks is a shopping list.

- Twos will choose to use their hands and fingers for some kinds of mark making, but their physical skills now enable them to exercise more confident control of brushes, thick crayons or chunky chalks and other mark-making tools. Older twos may want to have a go with a pencil or biro, although they are likely to hold it in a fist grip, rather than by fingers.

If you look back over this list of possibilities, you can see how young children's physical development goes hand-in-hand with their opportunities for creative expression: art and craft – two-year-old style.

Playful learning

Young skills are hindered, not helped, by being pushed into handwriting exercises, flash cards or letter drills. It takes time for these symbols to have real meaning for children. Such early pressure actually undermines the necessary physical confidence. Large physical movements are just as important for the later skills of writing as finer coordination.

- Large movements, such as playing with ribbons or large swirly movements with brushes, are important to hone the balance and skills that enable children to control pencils later.

- Trying to get two-year-olds to trace letters or other 'handwriting practice' displaces all the essential skills practice. The other negative consequence is the

high risk of convincing young children that writing is something very boring that adults make you do, for no obvious useful reason.

- Many creative activities build the skills for writing (much later – when children are ready). Very young children like to wield a paint brush, large crayon or chalk and make marks in whatever way they like. The practice builds the basis for the physical skills.

It is worth reflecting on the environment you provide and what sense it will make for the growing understanding of twos in terms of secure foundations for literacy. Look at any written material in your nursery – or in your home if you are a childminder:

- Is the writing there for a practical reason? Does it effectively say: 'Read me. I say something useful'?

- What about single letters on friezes, bricks, fixed to plastic toys, on quilts – anywhere? If single letters do not say anything at all, why are they there?

- When children become genuinely interested in letters, then they are better served by plastic or magnetic letters that can be moved around and held.

Look at how twos become absorbed in their self-chosen play, both indoors and outside. They are happy in what

PARTNERSHIP WITH PARENTS: PLAY RESOURCES

An important part of being a helpful practitioner to twos is sharing ideas and understanding with young children's parents.

Families are under pressure to buy their children 'educational' toys made of moulded plastic, battery-driven and in bright primary colours. Some of this expensive kit is flagged as suitable for two-year-olds, even sometimes for babies. These toys do not teach children how to talk and they do not teach phonics – no matter what it says on the packet or manual. When you see the extent to which letters (and numbers) are stuck to so many toys, it is hardly surprising that some parents quiz nurseries or childminders about when their two-year-old is going to know their alphabet.

Hold tight to your child development knowledge and do not be persuaded that partnership means you have to say, 'how soon would you like?'. A better, more professional response would be: 'I'm so glad you care about early literacy – so do I/we. Please let me show you what I/we do'. Settings or childminders who find ways to say and show this, usually find that parents then say, 'ah, now I see what you mean'.

LOOKING CLOSELY AT TWOS

I spent time with Ben (2yrs, 6mths) in his own home. He was a busy little boy, keen to show me his play resources and what he could do with them.

These observations show his fine physical skills relevant to his learning journey towards using tools for writing. You will also see evidence of other areas of Ben's learning, such as his creativity for art and design. What else could you say about Ben's learning from these notes?

- Ben spent 15-20 minutes working with play dough on his own kitchen table. He was interested in a simple machine that his mother Louise had recently bought for him. A pressing mechanism squeezed play dough through one of a choice of shapes. Ben was intrigued to find out how the new machine worked and was willing to press hard to operate it, although it was easier for an adult to start the press.

- Ben liked making 'snakes' and used a range of plastic tools to work with the long shapes or other pieces of play dough. Ben used his language to explain and direct with, 'we have to make a snake first' and 'shall we make another one?'. He explained, 'I'm cutting it for you' and asked his mother, 'you put some eyes on' (the snake).

- Ben used his fingers, a knife, scissors and a pastry crimper. He looked carefully and lined up the tools to cut, poke holes and make a series of deliberate marks. He selected, held and used each tool with care and looked carefully to see what he had done, before continuing his chosen focus, or selecting a different tool.

they do – and that is enough for itself – but notice also how so much of their playful activity involves use of tools. When twos are busy concentrating with materials of their choice, you can see them practise all the physical skills and hand-eye coordination that they will later use for handwriting – when they are ready.

It matters a great deal that early years practitioners commit to supporting young children on their learning journey towards literacy. However, mastering the written format of any language is highly dependent on young children's confidence in their spoken language. This essential early stage is even more crucial for English, because it is a highly non-regular language. There are exceptions to just about every spelling rule.

Mathematics

Many first-hand experiences, appropriate for very young children, build a meaningful foundation for early mathematical understanding. Young twos and rising threes learn through play, conversation and their active involvement in daily routines. They need time, space and generous open-ended and natural resources. Twos can be very aware and interested in their immediate indoor and outdoor environment, noticing the familiar and unexpected aspects. This knowledge and understanding of their immediate world supports their growing intellectual grasp of how that world can be sorted, organised and described.

Making practical sense of mathematical ideas

Many, probably all, of the early mathematical concepts only make sense through comparison. Something or somebody may be 'big', 'fast' or 'heavy', but compared with what? Twos are increasingly able to connect spoken words with a simple mathematical concept. However, this change does not happen just with the passing of the months. None of these abstract concepts make sense to young children without plenty of

direct, first-hand (and first-feet) experiences during the earliest part of childhood, including their baby and toddler years.

Twos benefit from plenty of opportunities to move materials around to a purpose – their own plans and intentions – through building, piling up, putting things in and out, selecting items that are more likely to fit. Their actions, repetitions and variations around their own chosen play focus then provide meaning for simple language from an adult as play partner. You drop a few, timely comments about position or height into the conversation, without hijacking the play.

Young children learn a great deal through playful enterprises, but they do not exclusively learn through activities that adults would usually label as 'play'. Twos, just like three to fives, are keen to be involved in familiar routines. They warm to feeling like a trusted helper and genuinely learn from being part of organising a snack or tidying up the bricks. Sorting out plates and cups, sharing out food and realising when there is 'no more' are all important, practical examples of quantity. They are also genuine reasons for someone – more often an adult than a young two-year-old – to count 'how many' or assess 'how much'. Older twos will soon be part of this practical application of mathematical concepts.

LOOKING CLOSELY AT TWOS

Numeracy and any use of early mathematical ideas only makes sense within a child's familiar world, so observational examples that highlight direct experience of early mathematical understanding usually also show children's knowledge and familiarity with their own world.

Consider how the following examples shine a light on these young children's skills in any other of the seven areas of learning and development.

- In Buckingham's Nursery, practitioners allow generous time for meals and snacks, because these routines are valued. The twos enjoyed breakfast time with drink, raisins and breadsticks. The adult used practical language related to the routine, like 'have you had enough?' and 'do you want some more?'.

- Another adult said, at an appropriate moment, to one child 'where do your raisins go' and the child was able to answer 'in my mouth'. During breakfast several children became very interested in when they, as individuals, were 'gone', by covering their face with their hands.

- In Buckingham's Nursery I observed two children (twos) who persisted in taking the bowl in and out of the wooden play sink. They explored moving the bowl around, trying to fit it and pushing it through the space, so that it was no longer secure. One child experimented with putting the bowl on her head – it was a good fit.

- In the Windham Drop-in two-year-old Gary moved around with confidence. Sometimes his mother was close by, sometimes he was absorbed in play and she was across the room. Gary moved between the opportunities that were available. He spent some time with the mark-making materials set out on a table. He was equally interested to explore letting a wheeled toy run down a slope to his mother. He spent time emptying a container of keys, exploring many of them individually – looking and feeling.

The observations above were made indoors, but a considerable amount of learning happens when young children have generous time outdoors.

Over a summer spent visiting Buckingham's Nursery, I watched their children engaged in a wide range of enthusiastic outdoor pursuits. Look at page 33 for some further examples, which highlight twos' early mathematical understanding, as well as other areas of their development.

Twos will join your provision with a variety of prior experience and there is more than one way to fall into the category of being a 'vulnerable' two-year-old. Some young children may live in families where there are serious financial difficulties and other stresses. Yet, their parent(s) have been able to give their very young child time and attention, so that this two-year-old reaches you with a secure base of skills gained from being involved in ordinary daily routines within the family. Perhaps children have few conventional toys, but they have done a lot of cooking with their parent or grandparent, or are already a keen gardener. This young boy or girl, vulnerable in some ways, could well be developmentally more secure than a peer who has been left with the company of expensive technological toys or sat for ages in front of a large television screen.

Some of these directly appropriate experiences will be happening in children's own homes. Effective partnership with parents will mean that the key person is aware of how much many twos are learning at home. With some, not all, parents, it may be important to communicate how much of this experience is very supportive of early mathematical understanding. Less confident parents may believe that 'proper' learning only happens within designated early years provision. Support for learning at home is not always about early years practitioners sharing ideas or suggestions. Sometimes it is mainly about alerting committed parents to the significance of what they are already doing with their young children at home.

With a well-resourced learning environment, twos are able to select flexible materials, which they then organise. They categorise materials in ways that make sense to them. The approach used by individual young children becomes clear to adults when you observe what children are actually doing with materials, rather than becoming over-focused on what you, as the adult, hoped they might do. Children need this basic concept of sorting and matching as the foundation for any kind of categorisation that rests on concepts that seem self-evident to adults. Such ideas only seem 'obvious' because we have lived with the ideas – like shape or size – for a very long time.

As easy as one, two, three?

Twos begin to show simple understanding of some number names – most likely through familiar number rhymes. They have a basic comprehension of quantity through ideas like 'more', 'a lot', 'lots and lots' and 'no more'. Their assessment of quantity and relative amounts is led through the evidence of their eyes. It may be that they have not got as much of something as another child – or that they have the biggest pile and intend to hang on tight.

Even babies and toddlers seem to have a sense of 'not enough' and look puzzled when an item has failed to re-appear in a now-you-see-it-now-you-don't game. Under twos can be clear in indicating that 'something is missing' and maybe their certainty is led by alertness to 'same' or 'different'. Over the year that they are two, young children can become ever more adept at the actual counting. However, written numbers are just meaningless squiggles to very young children. They need to have a reliable grasp about counting, and good reasons to use numbers, before they are able to make sense of written numbers.

If adults – practitioners or parents – rush into asking young children about written numbers, the response from twos will be a puzzled look. Sometimes – as I have observed – two-year-olds try their very best to reply to an adult question that is currently nonsense to them. The patient expression – on the face of the child – seems to convey the message that at some point this usually coherent adult will get back on a more sensible track.

There are plenty of ordinary opportunities that arise in play with children. You count when they want to use their fledging number approach – whether is it snails, pretend farm animals or putting socks into pairs. For most play resources, there will be more than one item and children often spontaneously say that there are two wheeled trolleys or three watering cans – so a child can use another one. There may only be one copy of a favourite book. Tidying-up time in nursery is also finding time and the same opportunities present themselves in a family home. I recall getting my own children to search for 'the last two pieces of our seaside jigsaw' or 'the three spoons missing from our tea set'.

Rising threes may know the order of low numbers, perhaps that three is always less than four. Like many abstract ideas, older twos and young threes benefit from a personal link. A given number is, 'mine. I'm three' or, 'that's our number', as in their house or flat number. Rising threes and young threes can become alert to numbers all around them, like the letters in writing that they see indoors and on the street.

You help two-year-olds by responding to their interest, as well as voicing out loud when you need to use numbers for making a purchase, preparing food or cooking and finding a route.

LOOKING CLOSELY AT TWOS

During the enjoyable mornings I spent watching Ben (2yrs, 6mths) play in his own home, it was possible to see him using mathematical awareness around concepts that I did not hear him put into words.

- Ben was interested to build a single-brick-wide tower. He added the plastic bricks one or more at a time. When the tower became wobbly from the height, he was content for me to hold it steady while he kept adding. I commented that it was such a tall tower. Soon the tower was too tall for Ben to reach to add more bricks, so he got a child-sized chair and continued to build. He seemed to understand what I was saying as I moved my hand to show 'nearly as tall as you/taller than you/even taller than you standing on the chair'.

- Ben worked confidently with his hands, for example fitting together the tracks of his train set (a simple round hole and shape lock). He fitted the train and trucks together and noticed straightaway if he did not have a hole and shape that would fit, turning the items around so that they would connect together. On this occasion, Ben did not voice his thoughts out loud but busily got on with building his track.

- Ben used his own words to describe a range of positional concepts, such as 'in', 'out', 'off', 'down' ('sit down') and 'under'.

- Ben used words like 'big' and 'little' correctly. He also showed a good visual check on size. For instance, he was able to look at the pretend French bread and say, correctly, 'that's too big' to put in his pretend toaster. But he judged correctly that the pretend slice of bread would fit.

- Ben also drew with his crayons, creating dots and lines in a deliberate way.

Meaningful numbers

You will support two-year-old understanding when you provide experience of numbers used for a practical purpose that makes sense to young children. Look at any numerical material in your setting, or in your home if you are a childminder:

- Are numbers there for a good reason? Can even twos begin to realise that this strange symbol says something useful?

- What about single numbers on friezes, bricks, fixed to plastic toys, on quilts – anywhere? The promotional material that comes with the toy or other resource may claim that the product supports very early numeracy learning, but what does your child development knowledge tell you?

- Some single written numbers are used for a good reason, because they are the number on the front door or the parking bay for bikes. However, if single numbers do not communicate anything meaningful, then why are they there?

- When children are genuinely interested in numbers, then they are better served by plastic or magnetic numbers that can be moved around and held.

- It is also wise to keep plastic letters in a different container from the numbers. Young children go through a confused stage when they do not realise that there are two symbols. There is no need to make it tougher by muddling up letters and numbers in one container.

- What about a number frieze? Do children actively look at it and point, or is it just wallpaper? A book with items to count may work better, or a story where a group of cats or other items disappear one at a time and then re-emerge.

Written numbers may seem like a very obvious way of representing quantity, and other mathematical concepts, to adults who learned their basic numeracy a long time ago. Yet these squiggles are not at all obvious to young twos and still a mystery to many rising threes.

Before children can use numbers to measure and describe their world, they need to be confident about the abstract concepts they want to turn into numbers. Twos can be very busy directly experiencing 'high', 'heavy' and the many different meanings for 'big'. Their playful enterprises are the very best way for them to understand these ideas fully. They need plenty of first-hand experiences of the continuum between, for instance, tall and short or slow and fast. Then their later application of numbers will be well grounded in a much broader early mathematical understanding of their personal world.

LOOKING CLOSELY AT TWOS

- Tanith at just two years imitated her older brother in asking us what specific written words said. At this age she confused written letters with numbers; she believed all the marks 'said something'. She liked to say, 'one, two, three, four', but without reference to anything in particular.

- At two years, six months, Tanith could finger-point to count a small number of objects. She liked to count up to five and sometimes made it to ten. At just over three years, Tanith could reliably finger-point to count actual objects, like books or bricks, up to five or six or more. She was confident counting up to ten, but liked some help with an adult voice joining in from ten to twenty.

- At two years, six months, Ben had a clear concept of two and seemed to identify confidently what looked as if it was one and one more. He accurately said that there were two trains and used two correctly for other sets of two.

PARTNERSHIP WITH PARENTS: ADULT'S CONFIDENCE

Some practitioners, along with some parents, have serious doubts about their own mathematical skills. It seems acceptable to announce, 'I'm useless at maths', when the same people most likely would not say, 'I'm rubbish at reading'.

The enjoyment for adults in sharing the understanding of very young children is that it can lay the maths 'gremlins' to rest. Parents need to observe a good example from practitioners: in what you say out loud and how you behave. Be a good role model to the twos and their parents.

- Do children see you writing numbers or a simple mark tally for a reason? Do they see and hear you counting – for a practical reason?

- In the same way, do children see you in action as a mathematical thinker and a measurer?

- Do you voice out loud what you are doing and link counting words and actions?

- Do you take ordinary opportunities to show naturally why you need to count, measure or look closely to assess, e.g. 'will you all fit onto the bench?' and 'do we need more …?'.

Understanding the world

There are many ways of describing the natural, as well as the made or built, world and two-year-olds will have some of the vocabulary needed to describe the characteristics of the world. They will also start to address puzzling issues around time and place.

Learning through the senses

As adults we could benefit from an image in our mind of a young child with a quizzical expression on their face – maybe even a little frown – and the serious question from that child of, 'do you know and understand my world?'. Twos are interested, often fascinated, by their world. Yet, practitioners and parents need to tune-in to young knowledge and the enjoyment that can come to us when we are open to sharing a child's fresh outlook. Much of this adult respect and attention has to be led through informal observation of what children are actually doing and their chosen conversations, including their questions – whether asked in words or through a puzzled expression.

Over the year that they are two, children gain a larger vocabulary that enables them to describe qualities like texture, weight, temperature or colour. However, they reach this

understanding through practical experience, when the words can be connected with something that already makes sense. It is important that adults look for this connection of meaning – through young children's current interests and knowledge.

You will tune-in properly to two-year-olds when you pay attention to how they choose to experience their world and how direct first-hand experiences lead their understanding of abstract ways to describe that world. It is valuable to think in terms of learning through the senses.

- **Vision:** young children need to use sight to recognise and distinguish different colour and shades. They have to see the difference before they can assign a word to that colour. When the day closes-in swiftly during wintertime, two-year-olds can see the difference between light and dark and how adults need to put the light on.

- **Touch:** children need to feel textures such as rough, smooth, bumpy (which could also be experienced by riding over) and some temperature changes like warm, hot or cold. As well as seeing basic shapes and lines, young children often learn by feeling the curves of a ball or cylinder or the edges of a squared box.

- **Hearing:** children distinguish levels of volume with loud, noisy and quiet. They use hearing as well as sight sometimes to identify familiar aspects of their environment: 'It sounds like a bird' or that the rain is 'going pit-a-pat', as well as making visible puddles in the garden.

- **Taste:** they use the power of taste not only for nice and nasty, but to appreciate some of the subtle flavours of food and drink with crunchy or juicy. They also often have their own words like the nearly two-year-old (told to me) who used the word 'nippy' to cover sharp or sour tastes like lemon.

LOOKING CLOSELY AT TWOS

In Buckingham's Nursery I watched a sustained, hands-on experience with gloop for a small group of enthusiastic twos.

- The activity was a good example of an adult-initiated experience, in which these young children were fully involved in setting-up the experience. Even young twos were able to help get the covering on to protect the table and they felt the mixture at each stage. The adult working most closely with them added words like 'soft' as appropriate and led discussion about the blend with remarks like, 'let's see if we need some more water'.

- The children were delighted to get their hands into the mix and the adult was just as active in making her own movements with the gloop. Children became interested in how the gloop dripped off their arms and deliberately tried variations, saying, 'get some more'. The gloop got everywhere and one child was interested to have her picture taken – and be able to see straightaway the state of her face as the adult commented 'gloop all on your face, on your nose'.

This example also provides a timely reminder that an experience that engages children will support the buzz of their learning in more than one developmental area.

- These twos were learning about texture, feel and the qualities of a liquid, runny substance. But they were also keen to add to the mark-making tools that the adults had offered. Young children went to other parts of their room to choose their own mark-making tools – particular favourites were spoons and whisks.

- All the children were keen to make their own marks and patterns in the gloop – some with very energetic swirly movements – all supportive of meaningful mark making so important for early literacy.

- **Smell:** probably the most overlooked sense but important to young children who recognise a whole concept of 'smells like...'. They possibly do not get much further than variations around 'nice' and 'nasty', because adults tend not to have a wide vocabulary to describe different kinds of fragrances.

There is good reason to talk about a sixth sense, in terms of how children come to be aware of the messages from their own body. The terms 'proprioception' or 'kinaesthetic feedback' are both used to refer to this sense of bodily awareness: what your own body tells you and a sense of closeness and personal space in regard to others. This concept is also mentioned in the section about physical development – another reminder that learning is holistic.

Young children may extend their current experience of their immediate world by using sight to look up for a sense of 'high'. Yet, using their whole-body to climb up high or stretching up for something on a high shelf gives another dimension to their understanding. Cars can be seen to go fast on the road or a child can make a toy truck speed along the paving. But there is another level of whole-body understanding when a two- or three-year-old whooshes fast down the slide or runs from one end of the garden to another.

Very limited early experience, or the impact of some disabilities, can reduce or remove the information from

sensory experience. Young children need as much help and suitable equipment as appropriate, to close the gap as much as possible. Practitioners need specialist input – from their own SENCO or local advisors – to support disabled children who are learning without the help of one or more senses.

Experiencing familiar and unfamiliar

Very young children learn about the different features of their world through a considerable amount of varied experience and hands-on exploration. They need to connect words that stand for ideas to what they experience through their senses. Adult comments need to make a clear connection between what they say and the immediate experience for twos.

- When a child is playing with a set of dolls there could be good reason to say, 'yes, you've got the large doll not the tiny one.'

- Helpful adults drop the words into their communication at a time and place that gives direct meaning. You might say, 'the doll's clothes are really wet. Perhaps we had better squeeze them before we hang them on the line'.

- Twos, even young threes, need to be able to connect what you say with something that makes sense to them. You help by listening and then following the child's lead with, 'yes, look at that water! It's going down the drain so fast'. Or you comment on what the child is doing: 'That basket looks heavy – shall I take the other end?'.

- The concept of opposites only seems obvious to adults because you have lived with pairs like wet/dry or hot/cold for a long time. Two-year-olds usually get one half of an opposite at a time: for instance they focus more on 'big' than 'little' or on 'rough/scratchy' rather than 'smooth'. Then, as they get interested, they start to explore the opposite and may go for fine gradations such as 'very big' and 'tiny'. Once twos start to use 'very very very big', you know they are ready for a word like 'enormous'.

These kinds of direct, first-hand experiences mean that two-year-olds are able to connect the words they begin to use themselves with a personal past history of meaningful experiences. Their spontaneous use of words is often led, and accompanied, by their imitation of the correct word or phrase used by a familiar adult. Relaxed time for indoor and outdoor experiences means that two-year-olds are very interested to use their improved physical skills to explore a wide range of materials and they make sense of appropriate comments by adults.

Look back at the description on page 12 and 26 of the Rumpus Drop-in trip to their local park. I placed elements of that enjoyable trip within PSED and physical development, but the example could just as easily have gone into this section.

LOOKING CLOSELY AT TWOS

I spent time with Sophie (2yrs, 8mths), her mother Louise and baby sister Lucy (5mths). The family had moved house four weeks previously and Sophie was already well established in her new indoor and outdoor world. Sophie was very active in her garden, moving water in containers, watering flowers, pouring from her bucket as well as transporting water to her vehicle – a sit-on bus with a seat that would open to show the storage area underneath, which Sophie was busy filling with water. Sophie was able to move this vehicle by pushing or trundling with skill up and down the garden path. Her tricycle was a bit more of a challenge. She could work the pedals, especially with a bit of help with Louise pushing, but the trike was a tight fit on the garden path.

Sophie was interested in stones in the garden and at one point was ambitiously trying to lever out a paving stone. She suggested to her mother, 'you can get that out.' Louise explained that it was not possible to get out the paving stones, that they were cemented in and, 'cement is like glue'. Sophie accepted this explanation and found an acceptable stone in the earth.

Sophie understood and knew a range of colours. This line of conversation started with Sophie's interest in the daffodils in the garden and she knew they were yellow. She had become interested in her own and the family's colours. Sophie was keen to go through each family member and their favourite with Louise. Sophie then decided that my favourite colour must be purple – a sensible logical guess from the colour of the top that I was wearing.

Sophie spends part of her week with a childminder and both her minder and her parents make the effort to link together the parts of Sophie's personal world. This morning, Sophie and Louise re-potted her bean, which she had originally planted with her childminder. Louise explained that the bean needed a larger pot, 'because it's squashed'. Sophie was interested and helped in the re-potting. They looked at the roots and it was clear that the bean was struggling in the smaller pot.

Sophie is also learning about the wider world from her books. Later in the morning she wanted a book and chose *Rumble in the Jungle*. Baby Lucy was also part of this enjoyment of a story and was secure on one side of Louise's lap with Sophie on the other side. Louise read the story and Sophie was only too ready to tell us, without any prompting, about items on the different pages. She identified the colours on the title page and helped Louise to turn the pages.

The narratives of children's worlds

Communication really matters, and that adults follow the child's lead. Two-year-olds are able to recall past experiences and ask questions that show they remember. When you listen to what twos want to say, their words join with the actions you observe to bring your adult understanding into a two-year-old world: the flow of time, important places and people and what is worth asking a question about right now.

Until you know young children well, you may lack key items of information to make sense of their narrative.

- When they run out of words, young children supplement with body language. Continued partnership with parents is vital to enable you to fill in the gaps, even when you are a very attentive key person.

- Two-year-olds may want to tell you something interesting about their home life, or to tell their parents about an important event at nursery or with their childminder.

- Twos who are confident of the interest and time of their important adults will also sometimes request the retelling of a personal narrative – out of interest and sometimes to rework and lay to rest less happy events.

Best early years practice is to have tangible personal links for young children between the different parts of their life.

Children often have their own special box or basket in which they keep items important to them. A particular shelf or top of a low cabinet may be where children can place something special to them. It may be a single leaf or stone, which a child has picked up on the way to nursery or their childminder's home. When you show respect for such an item, you affirm a young child's personal world.

Children are far more likely to express interest in what you know about the world when you have shown active interest in what really matters to them.

The revised EYFS (DfE, 2012) has continued the sensible shift towards talking about young children's growing understanding of community, rather than implying that under-fives understand the abstract concept of culture – either their own or that other people. Positive approaches about equality in middle childhood will be supported by developmentally appropriate practice over early childhood.

Young children's understanding starts with their family: the immediate family members and extended family when children have close contact. This personal world includes twos' early years provision: their nursery or the home of their childminder. This home-from-home is an important part of the community that makes sense to very young boys and girls. It adds a growing understanding of the immediate neighbourhood of their family home and of their early years provision, if this is in a different locality.

PARTNERSHIP WITH PARENTS: SHARING HIGHLIGHTS

A two-way easy pattern of communication will enable parents to ask you to fill in parts of their child's week with which they are unfamiliar.

I experienced this situation in my own family when, at nearly two, Drew wanted to tell me about his day with his childminder. Something important had happened that he explained with: 'No Diane – so sad'. Drew's childminder was called Angela, so I was perplexed. I asked, 'who's Diane?' and 'what was so sad?'. Drew tried hard, but could only emphasise that there had been 'no Diane' and that was definitely 'sad'. I asked Angela the following day and she explained that Diane usually came to their street every Tuesday and sold fruit and vegetables out of the back of her van. Drew looked forward to this regular event of choosing produce from Diane and having a chat with her. On this occasion Diane's van had broken down, so 'no Diane'.

Can you recall similar events from your partnership with families?

LOOKING CLOSELY AT TWOS

A great deal of early learning for young children rests upon their sense of who is part of their personal world. Such an understanding starts young and is supported by experiences like one that I observed in Buckingham's Nursery.

- One adult was looking with several toddlers at the laminated photos of children and the practitioners who work in the room. They looked at one photo at a time and the adult asked, 'who's that?' or 'who could that be?'. The toddlers were looking around the room and sometimes the adult would explain that this child or adult was 'not here today'.

- These young children were at an early stage of linking the photo image with a person and this kind of adult-led experience made sense to them and was clearly enjoyable – from the expression on the toddlers' faces. All the young children had easy access to laminated photos of their family and pet, if they had one.

LOOKING CLOSELY AT TWOS

Ben, at two years, six months, showed a 'can do' outlook through many aspects of his development. He had a substantial working vocabulary and constructed sentences that included different types of words. His phrases were largely grammatically correct.

- Ben asked questions with confidence. He was ready to ask, 'what is happening?', 'where are we going?' and 'what's under there?'.

- But he also clearly recalled and talked about events in the recent past. He reminded his mother how they came to visit my home (nearly two weeks earlier) and Ben played with water and containers at my kitchen sink. Also, Ben returned to playgroup after a month's break, yet asked straightaway 'where's Mr Ben?' (the male practitioner who had the same name).

- Ben expressed his own wants and wishes but was also confident to share his knowledge. For instance, Ben showed me his toy fire engine and immediately made the link to real ones, saying 'they put out fires'.

- Ben understood everyday information and communication technology such as television and a remote control. He recognised audio tapes and knew how to use the controls of the music player in his playroom. Ben had generalised from familiar equipment and he recognised similar machines and equipment in my house. Ben was confident that he could work my remote control or that we could get the tapes to work.

- Ben understood that some of his toys needed batteries and that they stopped making the sounds if the batteries had run down. He also understood that he needed an adult to put the batteries into a toy.

At this time, an important part of Ben's personal world was that his mother was expecting a baby.

- Ben was proud to show me his new bedroom at the top of the house. He explained that his old bedroom would be for the baby. He then took me to that room and showed me the pram. Ben was able to explain that this equipment was 'for the baby – in Mummy's tummy'.

- Ben demonstrated how the cot mobile worked and re-arranged some baby items in the cupboard to his satisfaction.

- However, as Ben's mother told me, he did not currently believe that he ever was a baby, despite the collection of Ben baby photos in his bedroom. It is very usual that twos think this way; they are very grounded in the present.

Under normally happy circumstances, even young twos will have a secure sense of their family and their position in it. They may be puzzled about elements such as how people change over time, for instance that Granddad was once a little boy. Best early years practice is for the key person to come to understand individual children's family patterns and who is important to them.

- Twos' understanding and interest in their own family is often reflected in their pretend play. Sometimes you will observe young boys and girls play out their own bedtime routine with small play figures.

- This accurate reflection of real life will co-exist with two-year-old flights of fantasy, such as the small world firemen coming to tea, along with their fire engine.

- However, this kind of imaginative play shows you this child's understanding of the wider world. It is unlikely that young children will weave this kind of narrative without having seen the fire engine (or other exciting emergency vehicles) zooming along the street during their local trips, with family or with you.

- The life experiences of twos can vary significantly. Some vulnerable twos who join your provision may have had few, if any opportunities, to build their knowledge of the local neighbourhood.

Twos are often interested in the families of the other children.

Expressive arts and design

Young children can be very creative – in the full meaning of that word. Twos can be open-ended thinkers, shown by their actions and words, because they have not yet worked out that some things are not possible. Very young children enjoy the range of activities that are often described as creative: painting and mark making, singing and dancing. But their creativity is also shown through their flights of imagination and pretend play. All these aspects are represented in this specific area of development for the EYFS. However, I want to start with the importance of pretend play, because this exciting development is so closely linked with two-year-old language skills (a prime area).

Creativity in thinking and pretend play

Creative development is only partly fuelled by getting engaged in arts and crafts, as enjoyable as appropriate activities can be for twos.

- Creativity is also shown by the flexible thinking that enables twos to try several different ways to get their wheeled trolley around a tight corner.

- A creative two-year-old, in a well-resourced learning environment, is enabled to think 'outside the box', because nobody is saying, 'where do you think you're going with those!'. For instance, large cotton reels can be used for threading but also make a fine boundary fence for the animals.

- A good store of pine cones and corks can be any food that two-year-olds want for their pretend cooking. A large cardboard box can be absolutely anything and sometimes more than one thing at the same time.

Well informed early years practitioners create the indoor and outdoor learning environment that enables young children to engage in rich, sustained play. The adult task is then to watch, listen and realise how competent and creative these young children have become. If two-year-olds have experienced a happy very early childhood and enjoyable experiences, they will now know enough of their world to play around with reality. They can use their imagination and creativity to tell simple stories and to weave pretend into their play. They do not yet show the lengthy role play of threes and fours, yet this development will emerge later if practitioners have noticed and respected the two-year-old version of imaginative flights and pretend creations. Twos also use their skills of communication to direct their own pretend play through self-talk – look back at the example of Freddie on page 23.

Genuine young creativity

Support for young creativity depends a great deal on the kind of reflective early years practice that supports every aspect of young learning. Of course, adult ideas are valuable and they are expressed through your words, actions and how you make interesting resources available. An adult-initiated experience for children should always be offered with genuine choice and an adult who looks only too keen to have a go too. Young children will then gather round you like bees round a honey pot. There is something very awry with an adult-initiated activity if that adult has to persuade and cajole children to become involved. Of course, creative projects, for all ages across early childhood sometimes start with someone's idea or direct suggestion. The best adult ideas rest upon their knowledge of what has already interested, or is highly likely to interest, these individual children.

Young children learn from sensory experiences and most of them really like to get their hands stuck into play dough, to make real currant buns or see what happens when they tip water into the outdoor digging area. Toddlers and two-year-olds like to wield a paintbrush – even a medium size grown-up paintbrush with a bucket of water outside. They learn mark-making skills and show two-year-old creativity with tools like large crayons, chunky chalks, their own hands and different kinds of materials and tools.

Supportive practitioners let twos concentrate and explore. I have heard several examples recounted within my training days when confident practitioners described how they watched older toddlers and twos spend their entire time spreading glue carefully on their own hands. These practitioners understood the significance for children's development when even young twos chose to wait patiently for the glue to dry and then focused eyes and fingers to peel off each section of glue at a time. Nothing conventional, like a collage, was made that afternoon, but a great deal was done and learned. These same practitioners valued the time they took to explain to parents why the little piles of dried-up glue on display were significant to their children.

LOOKING CLOSELY AT TWOS

Twos and toddlers, who know each other well, play together in sustained sequences, to which they return day by day.

In Windham drop-in, Jamie and Sara (both two-year-olds) chose to play together most of the session. Jamie's mother explained that they were close friends and regularly played together in each other's family homes.

At the drop-in, their current play choice was to get a wheeled wooden carriage each, put a dolly or teddy in each one and then wheel them about in tandem on the outdoor decking area. They would stop from time to time, line themselves up on two outdoor seats, park the buggies and take out the dolls for a cuddle. They sat like that for a while, had a chat and looked at each other's dollies, then put the dolls back and headed off again for another walk.

They were completely absorbed and happily at ease with each other. At one point the wheels of the buggies locked with one buggy pointing forwards and the other backwards. The two children continued to walk, going 'beep-beep', although Jamie had to walk backwards.

At two years, six months, Ben's play in his own home reflected his knowledge of real, familiar life and his own powers of imagination.

- Ben used his language to start and continue all kinds of play. In his bedroom Ben began a game by explaining to me, 'I'm going to hide for you' and then 'I'm going to hide in there' (the wardrobe). Ben enjoyed the game, when I acted as if I did not really know where he was and expressed surprised when he appeared.

- Ben was busy with creative pretend play. He offered cups of tea to me and to his mother, remembering about milk and sugar. He set out a table for pretend tea with cups and saucers, plates and spoons in sets.

- He offered me some pretend bread. I said that I liked Marmite on my bread but not in my tea. Three times Ben joked and spooned pretend Marmite into my tea cup. Think about what that means: when a young child is able to joke in this way.

- Ben had Baby Sam – a small doll with his own pushchair, blanket and baby cup. He was careful with Baby Sam and asked me to sit the doll on my lap when we were building with Lego® bricks.

When twos are fully engaged, out of their own choice, then there will always be some kind of end result: an outcome that is meaningful to the child. However, there will not always be a neat, tangible end product. Sometimes, twos will tell you very clearly that this drawing or construction is finished and needs to be on display. It has to be their decision and choice. Certainly, twos no longer regard a painting or collage as their own if practitioners feel impelled to tidy it up beyond (with children's agreement) backing a very damp painting that will otherwise collapse. I have listened to sensible, reflective practitioners who have been provoked to rethink their practice by twos who failed to recognise 'their painting' on the display board.

Children of any age across early childhood should never be under adult pressure to make something that can be fixed to a wall, put on a shelf or given to the family to take home. Photographs, as well as conversation, are a much better way to show and share with families the genuine two-year-old creative activities. This option then easily encompasses the fine tower of bricks or incredible 'deep, deep hole' which twos have created.

Young children understand the idea that pictures represent events or made items and they are very pleased to have a permanent record through photos of something that matters to them. Nursery teams and childminders who use a camera all say that young children soon identify which of their own 'work' they want to have captured on film.

Making music and singing

An awareness of sounds and the flow of sound patterns in their own language(s) is very important for children to become confident talkers and listeners. However, you do not have to press twos into making music and singing. They are keen to get involved so long as any group singing time is kept small and personal. Young children also want familiar adults who are only too ready to join in spontaneous outbursts of song or respond to a request to have a particular song or rhyme right now.

Young children explore ways to make sounds by using simple tools including their own bodies. Babies soon produce their own trills of sound and discover the fun of blowing raspberries. Playful adults (or older children) join in and very young children soon realise that they come equipped with the best instrument of all – their own voice.

- Older babies and toddlers explore hitting and tapping by using the traditional wooden spoon and saucepan approach. They soon have the co-ordination to make sounds through shaking something. They make scraping sounds with their own nails, but toddlers can be adept with a stick run along railings or the fence.

- You do not need complex musical instruments. You can buy very simple sound makers, basic xylophones, musical shakers and small drums that can tapped by little hands.

LOOKING CLOSELY AT TWOS

Some special sessions may be supported by a regular visitor with additional musical experience. Or childminders may take young children to a music group. However, the aim is that you also learn from someone with more expertise and musical ideas. Never let it appear to the children, or their parents, that singing or music making is a very specialised activity best led by experts.

While I was working with the Grove House Infant and Toddler team, the whole centre was benefiting from regular times with a music specialist. Practitioners with the under-threes experienced new songs and music making. They were able to observe which possibilities the children appeared to like the best, so these could become part of the usual day.

Some adults – practitioners as well as parents – are self-conscious about their singing. But young children will never criticise your singing voice. Twos believe everyone can sing, like everyone can paint or dance. So, by all means, start with songs that leave you feeling more comfortable – and support uncertain parents in this way too.

In the early stages, children will benefit from seeing you play with enthusiasm with resources that are currently unfamiliar to them.

- You can also make your own 'instruments', using cardboard tubes or plastic bottles with different substances securely inside. The twos will help you with this construction work.

- Outdoor sound systems are cheap to make by fixing up small pots and pans or CDs on a washing line. Or use a wooden frame, like an old-fashioned clothes horse. Provide simple tools and batons for hitting the pans.

Babies and toddlers benefit from hearing a range of music played from CDs. Start with what will be more familiar to you and to these individual children's family background and then edge outwards. See what you all tune-in to – patterns of musical tradition vary around the world and adult ears are more attuned to familiar tones and patterns.

Very young children are open-minded in their musical tastes and they certainly do not need exclusively 'children's music', such as songs or theme tunes from age-appropriate DVDs or television programmes. You can use this source for some music, especially if you realise from a two's reaction that they like this tune – just not as your main source of tunes and songs.

Young twos often recognise songs and pieces of music.

PARTNERSHIP WITH PARENTS: EXPRESSIVE ARTS AND DESIGN

Perhaps some parents may find the phrase 'Expressive arts and design' a little odd to apply to two-year-olds. You can show what is meant by these words in a two-year-old world. The importance of singing together may be a practical way to start. There is also a natural link into your willingness to learn family songs or rhymes, or favourite pieces of music.

You can also share with families the importance of pretend play as a visible expression of young children's imagination and creative expression. If there is any doubt in some families, then explain simply that pretend play is not 'messing about' in a negative way. Be ready with anecdotes about what their son or daughter's play shows of young thinking.

Parents need to see a very good example in your provision of how young children flourish with a generous store of basic materials, often recycled, and simple dressing-up items. Young children do not need bought outfits, anymore than they need expensive art and craft sets.

LOOKING CLOSELY AT TWOS

Enjoyment of music and sound-making starts young and builds on the musical awareness of even babies.

Human babies seem to have an inbuilt sensitivity and interest in rhythm and tuneful patterns.

- In Buckingham's Nursery there is an enthusiasm for singing and simple music making from babyhood. So it was not surprising that the two-year-olds in this setting had a secure understanding about song and singing. They relished a chance to sing and had a range of opportunities within their normal days.

- The Tweenies team in Buckingham's Nursery had developed a special rhyme and song time for the twos. This created an enjoyable time when the children were sitting up to the table in the short period before their lunch arrived. The room team had a cloth bag containing a range of laminated pictures or items that were part of a familiar rhyme.

- Each child had a turn pulling out an item and they usually recognised the song or rhyme, making an announcement like, 'I got row row'. The adult helped with, 'It's Marie's turn' and 'what's this one?'.

Making sense of the development of twos

Assessment preparation checklist: points to consider

The revised EYFS for England (DfE, 2012) requires that a developmental assessment is undertaken within the early years provision which two-year-olds attend. As explained on page 6, the preference is that you gather the information relatively soon after children's second birthday. So, these brief developmental highlights focus on the young twos.

The individual pattern of a two-year-old's development will be affected by disabilities or chronic health conditions, which affect their energy levels and general well-being.

The 'Know How Guide' (National Children's Bureau, 2012) confirms that the EYFS Framework does not require the progress check to be completed in a prescribed or standard format. However, the progress check must cover the prime areas of learning and development. Here are some helpful points to guide you in each area.

Personal, social and emotional development points

- Do young twos look at ease and comfortable within their familiar surroundings and with familiar people?

  O It is not necessarily a positive sign that a two-year-old will 'go to anybody'.

- Do they show understanding of regular routines that are normal daily life for them?

  O It is normal twos behaviour to object, maybe strongly, to changes in how they think the day should run.

- Have they made close and affectionate relationships within their family?

  O Given sufficient time and attention, have they made a close relationship with you, as their key person?

- Are these two-year-olds alert and interested in their personal world?

  O Do they show recognition of landmarks and other familiar aspects of regular local trips?

- Do they look closely and imitate familiar adults, or other children?

  O Can you see their personal observations rerun through simple pretend play – even brief glimpses?

- Do they show social awareness of other young children, with whom they have regular contact?

O Confident twos start to play with others, especially if they can mix with slightly older children as well as age peers.

O They do not exclusively play alongside.

● It is unrealistic to expect young twos to manage turn-taking, or other play social skills, without friendly adult guidance.

O Does this two-year-old accept, even seek, your help?

● Does this two-year-old express a range of emotions, through actions and facial expression?

O Twos will not be able to regulate their own strong feelings, without adult help.

● You should be alert to any twos who appear angry, anxious or sad for much of the time – also young children who appear unable to trust adults to help them.

● Young twos will not yet use words to name their feelings. However, with adult support, you could see this development if you are assessing an older two- or rising three-year-old.

Communication and language points

● Can individual twos listen to what you say personally to them, so long as you first ensure you have their attention?

● Do they show by their actions that they understand a wide range of simple requests, relating to familiar events and routines?

● Do they show understanding of some simple questions, when your words have no additional clues, like pointing?

O These may be 'where...' questions about spotting familiar people of objects.

● Do these twos have a range of words, or very short phrases, which are understandable to a familiar adult?

O These spoken words may be personal versions and short phrases hard for an unfamiliar adult to comprehend.

● Do they use their existing vocabulary to find out more?

O Do they ask simple questions about what objects are called or the names of people or animals?

● Do they use their speech, as well as non-verbal communication, to show they recognise something is out-of-the-ordinary in their world? (Something surprising or of interest, not necessarily upsetting.)

● It is normal development that, over the year that children are two, they have a stop-start quality to their speech. Their flow is interrupted as they search for a word, or alternative way of saying what they want.

● Do they show recognition of the opening words or tune of familiar songs or music?

O Do they show recall of the words and actions, of familiar rhymes or chants – maybe also join in with the singing?

● Can you observe the beginnings of simple pretend play: with dolls or small figures and vehicles?

O Twos should have made this move into being able to represent their familiar world through imaginative imitation.

● Do they use their speech, even in a very simple way, to guide themselves out loud?

● Do they show an interest in books – shared personally with an adult or choosing to look on their own?

   ○ Do they recognise the words, repeating phrases or illustrations of a familiar book?

Physical skills and confident points

● With ordinary opportunities to play and move around their environment, young twos should definitely look stable on their feet.

● Are they confident movers, able to stop, start and avoid obstacles – most of the time?

● They should be steady walkers, but can they also show a turn of speed, as they run?

● Young twos – and even more the older twos and rising threes – should be adept at moving from one physical position to another, in ways that require them to manage their balance.

● Some twos will already look physically more confident than their peers.

● Can you notice this skill as they clamber?

   ○ Their climbing and developing jumping skills may be used on furniture, as well as 'proper' equipment.

● Can twos also bend or squat down, then straighten up again?

   ○ Can they manage this skill with something in their hands?

● Can they use their fine physical skills in chosen play, such as simple building with bricks, sorting out relatively small items and moving small world figures and other items?

● Can they make deliberate marks: with their hands and fingers, or with simple mark-making tools or brushes?

   ○ If twos have not yet experienced this opportunity, do they show the skills, given the chance?

● Are they curious about their world – using their physical skills, as well as communication, to explore what interests them today?

● So long as they have given time to practise, young twos show skills of self-reliance.

   ○ Can they manage some basic dressing, undressing and helping you with their toileting?

   ○ Do they feed themselves with hands and simple cutlery?

● Can you observe their physical dexterity as twos help out in simple domestic routines?

   ○ What does this observation tell you about their ability to recall the routine or organisation within a familiar environment?

Further resources

EYFS (2012) Statutory and guidance materials

The Department for Education website is a good one-stop shop for EYFS materials. See: www.education.gov.uk/schools/teachingandlearning/curriculum/a0068102/early-years-foundation-stage-eyfs.

This site provides access to:

- Department for Education (2012) 'Statutory Framework for the Early Years Foundation Stage: Setting the Standards for Learning, Development and Care for Children from Birth to Five' – this is the statutory guidance, including the safeguarding and welfare requirements, which applies to all early years provision up to and including reception class.

- Early Education (2012) 'Development Matters in the Early Years Foundation Stage (EYFS)' – the non-statutory guidance explaining the four main themes of the EYFS and providing some developmental steps along the way towards the early learning goals.

- National Children's Bureau (2012) 'A Know How Guide: the EYFS Progress Check at Age Two' – non-statutory guidance to support this statutory assessment, to be undertaken by the key person/childminder in a two-year-old's early years provision.

Books and websites

- Arnold, C. (1999) *Child Development and Learning 2-5 Years: Georgia's Story*, Paul Chapman Publishing.

- Arnold, C. (2003) *Observing Harry: Child Development and Learning 0-5*, Open University Press.

- Beckmann Visual Publishing *Baby It's you: the First Three Years* (DVD) (www.beckmanndirect.com).

- Blythe, S.G (2004) *The Well Balanced Child: Movement and Early Learning*, Hawthorn Press.

- Blythe, S.G (2008) *What Babies and Children Really Need: how Mothers and Fathers Can Nurture Children's Growth for Health and Well being*, Hawthorn Press.

- British Heart Foundation National Centre (2011) 'UK Physical Activity Guidelines for Early Years (Walkers)' (www.bhfactive.org.uk/homepage-resources-and-publications-item/280/index.html).

- Campbell, R. (1999) *Literacy from Home to School: Reading with Alice*, Trentham Books.

- Close, R. 'Television and language development in the early years: a review of the literature' (www.literacytrust.org.uk/Research/TV.html).

- Community Playthings, *Creating Places for Birth to Three: Room Layout and Equipment* and other useful resources on www.communityplaythings.co.uk

- Department of Health (2011) 'UK Physical Activity Guidelines' (Single page fact sheets, longer version from British Heart Foundation (see above) (http://www.dh.gov.uk/en/Publicationsandstatistics/Publications/PublicationsPolicyAndGuidance/DH_127931).

- Dorman, H. and Dorman, C. (2002) *The Social Toddler: Promoting Positive Behaviour* (book and DVD) The Children's Project (www.childrensproject.co.uk).

- Early Childhood Unit: 'Everyday Stories – working with children under three' on www.everydaystories.org.uk

- Early Education *Learning Together* (www.early-education.org.uk).

- Evans, B. (2002) *You Can't Come to my Birthday Party: Conflict Resolution with Young Children*, High/Scope Educational Research Foundation.

- Featherstone, S. (ed) (2008) *Again, Again: Understanding Schemas in Young Children*, A&C Black.

- Healy, J. (2004) *Your Child's Growing Mind: brain development and learning from birth to adolescence*, Broadway.

- High/Scope UK (DVDs) *The High/Scope Approach for Under Threes* (www.high-scope.org.uk).

- Hope, S. (2007) *A Nurturing Environment for Children up to Three*, London Borough of Islington.

- Hughes, A. (2006) *Developing Play for the Under 3s: The Treasure Basket and Heuristic Play*, David Fulton.

- Jabadao, undated, *Developmental Movement Play,* Jabadao (www.jabadao.org/?p=developmental.movement.play).

- Karmiloff-Smith, A. (1994) *Baby it's You: a Unique Insight into the First Three Years of the Developing Baby*, Ebury Press.

- Jones, M. and Belsten, J. (2011) *Let's Get Talking: Exciting Ways to Help Children with Speech and Language Difficulties*, Lawrence Educational.

- Learning and Teaching Scotland (2010) *Pre-birth to Three: Positive Outcomes for Scotland's Children and Families* (www.ltscotland.org.uk/earlyyears/).

- Lindon, J. (2006) 'A sofa full of talkers' In Featherstone, S. (ed) *L is for Sheep: getting ready for phonics*, Featherstone Education.

- Lindon, J. (2009) *Positive Relationships in the Early Years: Parents as Partners*, Practical Pre-School Books.

- Lindon, J. (2010) *Positive Relationships in the Early Years: The Key Person Approach*, Practical Pre-School Books.

- Lindon, J. (2010) *Positive Relationships in the Early Years: Child-initiated Learning*, Practical Pre-School Books.

- Lindon, J. (2011) *Positive Relationships in the Early Years: Supporting Children's Social Development*, Practical Pre-School Books.

- Lindon, J. (2011) *Planning for Effective Early Learning*, Practical Pre-School Books.

- Lindon, J. (2011) *Too Safe for Their Own Good? Helping Children Learn about Risk and Life Skills*, National Children's Bureau.

- Lindon, J. (2012) *Planning for the Early Years: The local community*, Practical Pre-School Books.

- Lindon, J. (2012) *Safeguarding and Child Protection 0-8 years*, Hodder Education.

- Lindon, J. (2012) *Equality and Inclusion in Early Childhood*, Hodder Education.

- Lindon, J. (2012) *Understanding Children's Behaviour: Play, Development and Learning*, Hodder Education.

- Lindon, J., Kelman, K. and Sharp, A. (2008) *Play and Learning in the Early Years*, Practical Pre-School Books.

- Manning-Morton, J. and Thorp, M. (2006) *Key Times: a Framework for Developing High Quality Provision for Children Under Three Years Old*, The Open University.

- National Literacy Trust (http://www.literacytrust.org.uk/).

- Siren Films, *Attachment in Practice, Life at Two, Firm Foundations for Early Literacy and Two-year-olds Outdoors* (www.sirenfilms.co.uk).

- White, J. (2007) *Playing and Learning Outdoors – Making Provision for High Quality Experiences in the Outdoor Environment*, Routledge.

Acknowledgements

I have learned a very great deal over the years from time spent with children, practitioners, parents, early years advisors and college tutors.

I would especially like to thank the following people and places in connection with the ideas expressed in this book.

My appreciation goes to the early years advisory teams of Derby, Coventry, Hounslow, Lewisham and Richmond.

Many thanks to these settings for their warm welcome and letting me use observations in this book: Buckingham's Nursery School (Leek); Grove House Children's Centre (Southall); Mary Paterson Nursery School and Rumpus Drop-in (North London); St Mark's Square Nursery School (North London); Windham – a Partnership for Children (South London).

I also appreciate what I learned during my involvement with the What Matters To Children team and from working with Siren Films.

My thanks to the staff and parents of Crescent I Kindergarten, Grove House Children's Centre and Mary Paterson Nursery School for giving us permission to use the photos in this book.

I have changed the names of any children and adults in examples observed in actual settings. I have retained the names used by any author whose work I have referenced with brief examples. Drew and Tanith are my own (now adult) son and daughter and they have given permission for me to quote from the informal diaries I kept of their first five years.

My thanks to two families who gave permission to use observations of their children: Louise and Adam Gay (Lucy and Sophie); Louise and Kevin Browne (Ben).

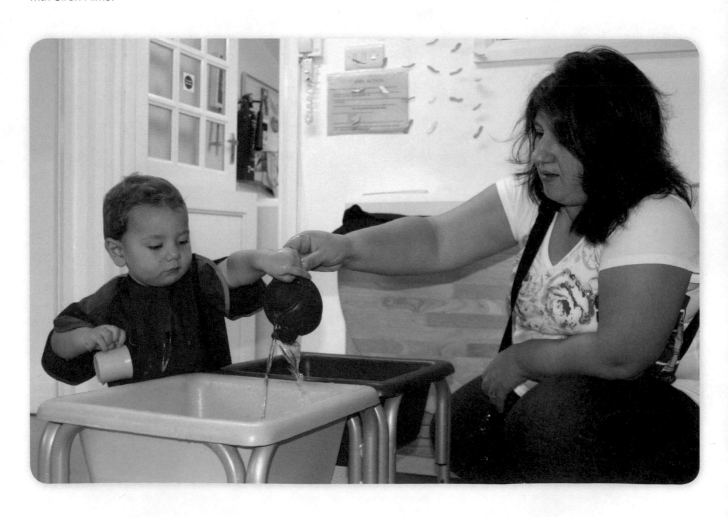